If you're struggling to rediscover your joy, read this book. Bev DeSalvo shares her own journey with poignant honesty, and she invites you to retrace your past in order to move into radiant hope. Bev gently guides the reader out from under the shadow of false shame and misplaced guilt and into to a place of embracing tears, practicing forgiveness, and dwelling in the place of God's light and hope. You'll benefit greatly from the powerful Bible study that accompanies each chapter. Buy one copy of *Return to Joy* for yourself and ten more to share with a small group of women who long to be free of the past in order to live triumphantly in the shelter of God's love.

CAROL KENT
Speaker and author of *When I Lay My Isaac Down*

A fervent follower of Christ, Bev DeSalvo takes you by the hand and guides you on a journey from brokenness to joy. With a passion to lead others to wholeness, Bev walks with you on the road of brokenness she herself has traveled. Steeped in Scripture and accompanied by meditative questions, this book will challenge you to lay aside the wounds of your past, embrace the healing and freedom found only in our Divine Nurturer, and return to a joy-filled journey. I pray that *Return to Joy* blesses you as much as it blessed me.

CYNTHIA HEALD
Author of the Becoming a Woman Bible studies

If you feel as though you'll never be happy again, this book is for you! Allow Bev to tenderly take your hand and show you how to find the path back to joy. No matter what hurt or trauma you've experienced, joy can be yours!

BECKY HARLING
Speaker, John Maxwell Certified Coach, and author of *The 30-Day Praise Challenge* and *Rewriting Your Emotional Script*

Many who have suffered through trauma are on a "healing journey." Yet God has more for you than healing—He invites you to travel the broken road to intimacy. Bev's powerful story testifies that God can work through your greatest pain to bring you into an intimate relationship with Him, your Creator and Lord.

DR. JULI SLATTERY
Cofounder of Authentic Intimacy

Return to Joy is a journey of hope and healing. Bev DeSalvo shares honestly about the sexual abuse of her childhood. She then invites Jesus into the depth of her pain, and His healing love produces a deep passion for Him. All her wounds cry, "Alleluia!" In the midst of suffering comes a depth of worship that is contagious. I have ministered in conferences and prisons for many years and have been waiting for this book. It is a powerful gift to those suffering pain and seeking peace.

LINDA STROM
President and founder of Discipleship Unlimited and author of *Karla Faye Tucker Set Free*

Bev DeSalvo honestly shares her journey from childhood pain and abuse to the healing arms of Christ. *Return to Joy* is a story of courage and hope. This book will take you to the feet of Jesus, where you will receive a garment of praise for a spirit of heaviness.

TERRY MEEUWSEN
Cohost of *The 700 Club*

Return to Joy is a helpful resource for Christians who have been wounded through childhood or adult trauma or loss, particularly if they wish to experience greater intimacy with God. De Salvo takes seriously the impact of such wounds and does not offer easy solutions. She does, however, offer concrete suggestions for a step-by-step process that can lead individuals into emotional and spiritual healing.

HEATHER DAVEDIUK GINGRICH
Professor of counseling at Denver Seminary

What a gift Bev has given us in *Return to Joy*. The unvarnished view into her deepest hurts, the wisdom gained through pain, the secret to unfettered joy. Read this book and join others in studying it together. It will enrich your life.

JENNIFER KENNEDY DEAN
Executive director of The Praying Life Foundation and author of *Live a Praying Life* and other books and Bible studies

Finding Healing
in the Arms
of Your Savior

RETURN
TO
JOY

BEV DESALVO

A NavPress resource published in alliance
with Tyndale House Publishers, Inc.

NAVPRESS

NavPress is the publishing ministry of The Navigators, an international Christian organization and leader in personal spiritual development. NavPress is committed to helping people grow spiritually and enjoy lives of meaning and hope through personal and group resources that are biblically rooted, culturally relevant, and highly practical.

For more information, visit www.NavPress.com.

Library of Congress Cataloging-in-Publication Data

Names: DeSalvo, Bev, author.
Title: Return to joy : finding healing in the arms of your Savior / Bev DeSalvo.
Description: Colorado Springs : NavPress, 2016. | Includes bibliographical references.
Identifiers: LCCN 2016003096| ISBN 9781631465406 | ISBN 9781631465413 (e-pub)
 | ISBN 9781631465420 (kindle)
Subjects: LCSH: Pain—Religious aspects—Christianity. | Suffering—Religious aspects—Christianity. | Spiritual healing. | Healing—Religious aspects—Christianity. | Joy—Religious aspects—Christianity.
Classification: LCC BV4909 .D44 2016 | DDC 248.8/6—dc23 LC record available at http://lccn.loc.gov/2016003096

Printed in the United States of America

22	21	20	19	18	17	16
7	6	5	4	3	2	1

To my Beloved,
Who has graciously helped me return to joy.
And to His wounded children.

Contents

Acknowledgments

SPECIAL THANKS TO

My incredible husband, Gary. Thank you for loving me as I walked the broken road to healing. I celebrate each day we have together as a treasure.

My cherished family. You are a priceless gift from God, and there are no words to express my love for you.

The amazing women who field-tested this study, including DeAnn Martin who has been faithfully by my side in each class. You have been my heroes, constantly encouraging me each step of the way.

The brave men and women who shared your stories. Your pain is being used by the Holy One to bring hope and healing to others.

The precious women of Temple Bible Church, past and present. You have been my spiritual family, and I thank God for you.

The two special women who walked the grueling healing journey with me, Linda Dillow and Kris Hungerford. Thank you for being God's loving arms to hold me when my life fell apart. My heart is forever bound to yours, tied with a divine knot.

My cheerleaders, Cynthia Heald, Linda Strom, Lorraine Pintus, Nanci McAlister, Nancy Winburne, and Sandi Funkhouser. You have faithfully reminded me that God can use my pain for His glory.

The talented people at NavPress, especially Don Pape, Caitlyn Carlson, and Karen Lee-Thorp. God has used you to bring my dream to reality, and it has been a great joy to work with you.

Foreword

WHEN WAS THE LAST TIME you read a book that was authentic, shocking, and hope-filled? You are holding such a book in your hands.

Authentic. Bev DeSalvo is one of the bravest women I know. Bev had correct biblical answers for others until her own hard questions began to surface and her neatly packaged world began to fall apart.

She says things a Christian leader doesn't say and admits to weaknesses senior pastors' wives never admit to. Bev's authenticity is refreshing!

Shocking. I grew up in a dysfunctional home, but life with my abusive alcoholic father was mild compared to Bev's distorted, dysfunctional home. Sexual and emotional abuse burned lies like these in Bev's heart:

- I am unwanted and will never belong to anyone.
- I can't trust God or anyone else because no one protected me.
- If people really know me, they will hate me.

Hope-Filled. My heart fills with hope as I read *Return to Joy* because God gave me the great privilege to walk with Bev through her healing. I watched her grow as a worshiper and embrace God as her Abba. She had always loved Him, but I saw her fall in love with Him. As she forgave the most difficult things to forgive, as she learned to fight against the enemy in practical ways, I marveled. The lies the enemy branded on Bev's soul have been replaced with God's truth. It is beautiful to behold!

I remember when Bev said to me, *"Linda, Satan desires to use my pain as a barrier to keep me from trusting God and others. But when I bow my pain to the Holy One in worship, He will use it as a magnet to draw me to His heart."*

This book will fill you with hope because you will see step by step how Bev faced her fears and moved from a "polite" relationship with God into captivating intimacy with Him. And you will learn how this precious woman who couldn't trust in relationships moved from "light" friendships into deep, intimate friendships.

Whether you come from a wonderful Christian home or a not-so-wonderful home, this book will challenge and encourage you! I already have a list of ten friends who are receiving *Return to Joy* as a birthday gift!

Linda Dillow
Author, Calm My Anxious Heart

The Journey into Broken

Not to us, O LORD, not to us,
   but to your name goes all the glory
   for your unfailing love and faithfulness.

PSALM 115:1

ONCE UPON A TIME, my life appeared to be almost perfect. I had been married to the love of my life for twenty-four years, had a married daughter and a son in college who both loved the Lord and enjoyed being with the rest of the family, spent time with great friends who loved to spend time with me, took exciting ministry trips to places all over the world—what more could anyone want? I was happy, or so I thought. I rarely cried or felt depressed—and yet something was wrong. No matter how wonderful everything appeared to be on the outside, a part of me felt lonely and afraid.

As director of women's ministry at the church where my husband is the senior pastor, I had the privilege of leading over sixty leaders in a thriving ministry. Hundreds of women were involved in vibrant and enriching activities. I had daily quiet times, counseled women, and taught Bible studies. I had all the correct biblical answers . . . until my own hard questions began to surface and my neatly packaged world began to fall apart.

I've always been fearful of deep intimacy, for reasons I'll go into later—and yet I've also had an unquenchable yearning in my soul for something more in life. But I made every kind of excuse to avoid dealing with my wounds. *Counseling is too expensive.*

Working on this will be painful and take too long. People may think I'm weak. I was appalled at the thought of becoming vulnerable and needy.

And then the Holy Spirit began wooing me down a broken road. Crushed with grief, I walked a path toward healing filled with the potholes of my past and obstacles of hopeless despair.

Even though I am a Southern woman through and through, God took me to Colorado for counseling. For three days in a row, three excruciating hours each day, I met with Kris, a biblical counselor, and my new friend Linda Dillow. It was horrifying to open up my box of pain alone, much less in front of them. The first memory, the one I had guarded for over forty-five years, slowly unfurled. Curled up in the fetal position in the arms of women I hardly knew, I wondered, *When will this be over?*

By the end of the last session I had decided I would never put myself in a grueling situation like that again. As the three of us walked down the hall to schedule my next counseling session via telephone, I concocted a lie so that I could politely bow out. "Before I make any more plans for counseling, I need to talk to my husband," I told them confidently. But I didn't want to ever set foot in that dreadful place again.

Within a few weeks, however, more memories began to surface. My seemingly perfect world began to crumble. I became engulfed in heavy sorrow . . . so much so that I felt like I was going to die. The only place I knew to turn was back to Linda and Kris. Their support over the following years, along with the encouragement of a few other close friends and family members, was a crucial part of my healing journey. Without them, I can't imagine what I would have done. So, like Abraham, I stepped out in faith onto a broken road and went without knowing where I was going (Hebrews 11:8).

We all have broken places, and we all have a compelling desire within our hearts for healing and wholeness, but it takes incredible courage to begin walking the broken road to intimacy. This is where all walls come down and you can enjoy an intimate relationship with God and others. Taking those initial steps can be so frightening and painful that we usually quit before we have a chance to find restoration. The lies in our head tell us, *This road is too hard and too long. I'll never make it to the end.* However, there is One beckoning us: Draw near. Trust Me, and you will find that the journey will be worth it. You will find rest and comfort in My embrace.

MAKING THE JOURNEY

This journey may sometimes feel winding and hard. If you choose to come along, you may find yourself asking the question, *Where am I going?* Together with our Savior we will walk through the Valley of Weeping and into the Gateway of Hope. We will come to truly know and understand the Father in the Secret Place, Jesus along the Bridge to Romance, and the Holy Spirit as we find comfort Under His Shadow. We will learn to fight against the lies from the evil one as we descend into the Shadow of Darkness, and we will find healing in the Place of Forgiveness. In the Garden of Gethsemane, we will come out of our hiding places and find hope in community—and ultimately, we will find ourselves in the Shelter of the Most High, where we will learn to rest.

In this book, we will face hard questions together. Each chapter includes a weeklong Bible study to help you engage more deeply in your journey toward healing and find hope and insight through daily time with the Lord in His Word. This study can also be used in a small-group context, and I have provided a facilitator's guide at the back of the book to lend insight and perspective about how to lead this material in community. Great healing can happen when we come together and realize we are not alone on this broken journey.

Even though the road is uncertain, the Father promises that He will ultimately lead us into His loving embrace, where emotional and spiritual healing take place. He has healed my broken heart, and it is my prayer that you, too, will find healing in your Savior's arms as you begin walking the broken road to intimacy.

> The LORD directs the steps of the godly.
>   He delights in every detail of their lives.
> Though they stumble, they will never fall,
>   for the LORD holds them by the hand.

PSALM 37:23-24

CHAPTER I

WHY THIS JOURNEY?

ONE OF MY EARLIEST MEMORIES was when my mother hurled a peanut butter jar across the room at Dad in anger. I remember his face turning red and his eyes narrowing into an all-too-familiar look of rage as he screamed at her, "I'm going to kill you!"

I was the fourth of five children with an abusive father and an emotionally distant and manipulative mother. My parents had screaming fights that frequently became violent. Naturally I was petrified each time one of these violent outbursts occurred. Because of my gentle temperament, I tried to be the "peacemaker" in our family. Even though I was a small child, I became an expert at reading body language, and I did everything within my power to encourage harmony. Putting on a mask and making people laugh became a way of life for me. I took on a huge burden that was impossible to carry and should never have been my responsibility in the first place.

My father may have been short in stature, but he made up for his size with his physical strength and commanding influence. I was terrified of his temper, but my mother was not. Her strong-willed determination never allowed anyone to get the best of her.

She and Dad seemed to be having a contest to see who could scream the loudest and insult the other with the harshest words.

Dad had a mental condition called borderline personality disorder, which is characterized by long-term patterns of turbulent emotions that result in chaotic relationships. He struggled constantly with inappropriate anger and extreme jealousy that escalated into physical fights on many occasions. He vacillated between idealizing my mother or me and my siblings one moment and then abruptly shifting to fury and uncontrolled violence over a minor misunderstanding the next. I lived in a constant state of terror, knowing that Dad could go ballistic in a flash, screaming curses and physically abusing anyone who got in his path.

Running to my hiding place one evening, I could hear my dad screaming, "Who saw Satan destroy my slippers?" (Satan was our German shepherd.) Gripped with fear, I crouched in the corner of my closet, waiting for the explosion and trying my best not to breathe for fear that Dad would hear me.

On another day I heard the thunderous blast of a gun. Dad had become outraged when my sister, who was eleven years older than I, came in after her curfew. In a moment of insanity, he picked up a gun and fired a shot above her head. Somewhere inside me, a tiny voice whispered, *Is this normal?*

In the midst of all the craziness, I have a few good memories of my dad. I was two years old when my baby brother was born, and my father helped more with caring for me. Rocking in Dad's lap while watching television became a nightly ritual. But I was taught very little about real love—love that is safe and supportive. Instead, as I became my dad's favorite, a trauma bond formed. This type of bonding occurs when one person exerts control over another, causing the other person to feel intimidated, confused, harmed, or diminished in some way. At times I felt like I was on a roller coaster, doing almost anything to stay in my father's good graces. I experienced glorious highs when the agony of his wrath was temporarily relieved. During these precious moments, I thought, *Is it possible that he really loves me? Maybe I can keep him happy if I try really hard.* But of course those feelings of euphoric relief never lasted. Without fail, Dad would blow up over some trivial incident and I would come crashing down emotionally. This insecure attachment made it hard for me to be able to hold on to love or have healthy boundaries. I desired comfort from others but avoided intimacy because I was deeply afraid of being hurt.

As bizarre as it sounds, my mother considered Dad's outrageous behavior normal when it was directed toward someone other than herself. In fact, his temper was her most powerful weapon against my siblings and me. When she was upset about something, she would convey it to my father in a way that could make him morph into a madman. He would come ranting into my room, ready for a fight, and my heart would pound as I waited for the back of his hand to smack my face.

When we disagreed with my mother in any way, she would shut down emotionally, but her silence spoke louder than words. Then, like a surprise thunderstorm that comes rolling in, some small incident would set her off. Without warning, she would barge into my room in a screaming rage and then slam the door as she left. As soon as I breathed a sigh of relief, she came storming in again. In the midst of her outrage, I stared blankly at her face without speaking a word.

Without a doubt, my mother wound was my deepest heartache. My greatest desire was to have a mother who treasured me. While Mom did a good job providing meals, clean clothes, and the basic essentials, she demanded my undivided devotion and was jealous of my relationships with everyone else, including my dad. She constantly tried to pit all of us against each other.

Mom's erratic behavior caused me to become extremely anxious about pleasing her. The only way I could fall asleep at night was by fantasizing about Mommy, the mother of my dreams, coming to my rescue. In my mind, Mommy held me in her loving arms and kissed my tears away. When I was naughty she gently disciplined me, but never without holding me and assuring me of her love. I wasn't invisible to her. Mommy was the most wonderful mother in the world. But while daydreaming provided some comfort, it never lasted.

I should have known that something even more tragic had happened to me because there were too many perplexing things that didn't make sense. Unfortunately, when that's all you've known, it's hard to know what is normal. But a few years ago I began to remember some unspeakable sexual things that were done to me when I was very young by someone who should have protected me. My mind had fractured into pieces that carefully guarded the horrific secrets so that I could survive. I grew into a woman with a mature body . . . but there was a huge wounded part of me that never grew up.

The trauma of my childhood caused me to experience what I call I-want-to-die kind of pain. Unfortunately, some of you know exactly what I'm talking about. The first time I remember wanting to die was when I was about ten years old. I can't remember what happened to cause my devastation, but I was without hope. Sitting in the tree house that I inherited from my older brother, I prayed, *Please help me, God. Nobody wants me! Everyone would be better off if I was dead.* I had seen some poison in the garage and wondered how much it would take to kill me and how much it would hurt. Would I go to hell if I drank it? That was the first of countless suicidal thoughts I struggled with over the following years.

I attended church only on very rare occasions as a child, so spiritual things were confusing to me. When I was about seven years old I prayed: *God, I'm really afraid to die because I do lots of bad things. It's okay if You don't want me. I understand.*

When I was nineteen years old, however, I was invited to attend a college outreach where I heard about someone who loved me so much that He was willing to die for me. This was what I had been longing for all of my life—someone who would love me unconditionally. I believed that I was a bad girl, damaged beyond repair, so this seemed like an irresistible offer—but terribly risky at the same time. I desperately wanted to trust Him, but I was terrified that I'd be hurt again. Despite my apprehension, I very cautiously entered into a relationship with Jesus Christ, and miraculously, He accepted me with all of my doubts and concerns. Unfortunately, I brought along with me the baggage of my broken childhood.

Thrilled and yet puzzled to be a new Christian, I felt like I was a black sheep—in God's fold but different from all the rest. I had no idea how I was supposed to act. Desperate to understand, I began pouring myself into studying God's Word. I read everything I could get my hands on and gained a lot of head knowledge, but there was always something missing. No matter how much success I achieved, or how many people told me they loved me, I still felt lonely and unlovable in the depths of my heart. I believed with my head that Jesus' blood covered my sin, but in my heart I felt dirty because of the awful things that had been done to me and the awful things I'd done as a result.

JOY STOLEN

The strongest force in the first two years of a child's life is the desire to experience joy in loving relationships. Finding comfort from a nurturing caregiver in the midst of pain brings restoration to a child's emotional balance, and the child is able to get down and play as if nothing painful ever happened. Psychologists call this returning to joy.[1]

I never learned how to return to joy when I was hurt as a child. For many of us, lack of nurturing continues to impact our ability to hold on to joy. Why is it so hard to move past our pain? Why do we sometimes struggle to change our thinking as we mature and move further from our abusive pasts? Here is the truth: As believers, we have an enemy far more powerful than those who have hurt us.

One of the biblical names given to Satan brings greater understanding of his true nature. He is repeatedly called the evil one (Matthew 6:13; John 17:15; 1 John 2:13-14; 5:18-19). This evil one deceptively uses all of the harsh things in our lives to destroy our innocence and define what we believe about ourselves and others. He brands lies into us that act as a barrier to keep us from trusting anyone, especially our heavenly Father.

Carefully consider the following "big little lies" that I've struggled with to see if you can identify with them:

I am a detestable piece of trash. Actually, that is the cleaned-up version. Whenever I did something that upset my mother, she would blurt out an expletive. In time, I believed that she was upset with who I was rather than what I'd done. Hearing this over and over again made me feel like I was worthless. Has anyone ever made you feel like rubbish? Even if those exact words weren't used, being ignored or treated as if you have no value can cause similar thoughts to penetrate your mind.

I am unwanted and will never belong to anyone. I felt like something was terribly wrong with me because my parents didn't seem to want me. I developed an orphan mentality, identifying with real and fictional children who had no parents or parents who didn't want them. I was lonely and afraid and felt like I didn't belong to anyone. Have you ever felt like you didn't belong? You may have grown up in a loving family, but Satan can use many different methods to make us feel lonely and isolated.

I can't trust God or anyone because no one protected me. I couldn't understand why people who should have loved and protected me hurt me instead. More importantly, I wondered where God was when those bad things happened. Because of this I became strong and independent. I was afraid to need or want anyone because it was excruciatingly painful when they let me down. Are you afraid to trust others because of painful experiences in your past? Have you ever wondered where God is when bad things happen? Satan is the victor when we lose trust in God and the safe people He brings into our lives.

If people really know me, they will hate me. Since I had been prematurely awakened sexually, I had no healthy boundaries, which allowed people to take advantage of me. As a result, I lived a life of duplicity. I was a good girl who tried to please everyone, but I also had a hidden side that lied and did sexual things to myself and others. I believed that if anyone knew the real me, they would be disgusted. Have you hidden your true self in shame because of sinful actions done to you? Have you ever wondered why you acted out sexually? Satan uses sexual trauma to make us believe shameful messages about ourselves.

I need to hurt myself. From the time I was a small child I believed I deserved to be punished. As a result, I began peeling my fingernails into the quick until they bled. It sounds absurd, but this soothing pain was strangely comforting. At times I still struggle to keep from hurting myself. In a way, I am addicted to pain like an alcoholic who craves the numbing effect of a drink. Are you ever tempted to hurt yourself in some way, like cutting or starving yourself? Do you feel that you need to be punished for something you've done or something that was done to you? Self-inflicted pain may bring comfort for the moment, but it never lasts.

I hate myself and want to die. Over the years I have thought of hundreds of ways to take my life. In this state of irrational thinking, I honestly believed that everyone would be better off if I was dead. Have you experienced I-want-to-die kind of pain? Or perhaps you simply wish that Jesus would return today. This is one of Satan's greatest lies: that we can't experience supernatural healing until we are in heaven.

I've shared my story with women of all ages around the world, and even though their experiences have been different from mine, all of them can identify with some of these lies. In fact, one college-aged woman admitted that she grew up in a loving Christian home, yet she could identify with every one of them. This tells me that Satan is crafty but not creative. He uses different methods but always with the same purpose: to keep us from trusting God and other people.

AVOIDING THE JOURNEY

We all have experienced painful things in life that cause us to struggle with lies about God, ourselves, and others. Perhaps you think that your pain is nothing compared to mine, but pain is pain. Unfortunately, merely coping with the pain will never be enough, and avoiding God's invitation to the broken road will result in even more pain.

Even when unrecognized, emotional trauma can create lasting struggles in an individual's life. My siblings tried various methods to deal with their pain. My oldest brother tragically snuffed his pain out. Raging with uncontrolled jealousy, he murdered his wife and then committed suicide. Because he left no note, our family was saddled with gut-wrenching questions. What could have made him do something so violent?

My older sister spewed her pain out on others. Haunted by borderline personality disorder and alcohol addiction, she became a troubled woman with rage-filled insanity. We never knew when, where, or how her anger would erupt, but we knew it was inevitable. She died a few years ago from cancer and alcohol-related problems.

In my lifetime I have tried a variety of methods to deal with pain. I have tried to fight against it, stuff it down, snuff it out, use it, abuse it, kill it, sleep it away, sweep it out, shop it up, and soothe it with relationships. About the only thing I didn't do was feed it. Instead, I have a tendency to starve my pain. When I'm upset I lose my appetite and begin to lose weight. Feeling the bones in my chest and having my clothes fit loosely feels right in my skewed thinking. But because I want to take care of God's temple, which is my body, I now work hard to maintain a healthy weight. All of these coping methods are only temporary fixes and can never bring true healing.

Even professional counseling, as critical as it was, simply helped me know a little more about why I was struggling—I still didn't know how to fix it. My response? I stuffed all my pain down inside and lived my life behind a mask. After all, a good Christian isn't supposed to feel sad, mad, or bad, is she? In order to keep this facade up I had to protect my heart from being hurt by people. But a hardened heart meant that I couldn't experience true intimacy with God.

Hiding our emotions will never work—they always find a way to come out. Sometimes these responses can be delayed, for months or even years after the event. Here are a few ways trauma might manifest itself:

Physical problems. Research has established that living in a constant state of anxiety can impair the development of the brain and nervous system. As a result, the body can be affected in various ways, including eating problems; sleep disturbances; sexual dysfunction; stomach problems; low energy; and chronic, unexplained pain. As a child I experienced stomach problems that developed into a debilitating colon disease that required four surgeries. I've also had TMJ (jaw problems), depression, stress-induced tachycardia, and sleep problems. Have you struggled with any of these symptoms and wondered where they came from? Unexplained fatigue, headaches, or stomach problems could be the result of unresolved trauma.

Emotional problems. Trauma can create a loss of faith that there is any safety, predictability, or meaning in the world. This can result in depression, anxiety, panic attacks, attachment problems, compulsive and obsessive behaviors, the feeling of being out of control, anger, emotional numbness, and withdrawal from relationships. Do you struggle with any of these? Have you ever felt like you couldn't connect deeply with others or that you needed to control everything around you? Our ability to cultivate healthy relationships depends on our having first developed those kinds of relationships in our families. I've had a deep fear of intimate relationships for most of my life and have kept most of my friends at an emotional distance. I was surrounded by wonderful people but became uncomfortable if I began to "need" someone. Even though I had many friends and enjoyed frequent lunches and social engagements, I was lonely on the inside.

Spiritual problems. Evidence suggests that trauma can lead to loss of faith in God, anger toward God, fear of spiritual intimacy, and a lack of desire to be involved in religious activity. Have you been confused about the way you perceive spiritual things? Do you feel like your heart is hardened toward God at times? This was true in my life. Even though I longed for true intimacy with God, He seemed to be elusive and out of my reach. I had desperately studied the Word of God but was afraid to get too close to the God of the Word. I read through the Bible many times and prayed through the Scriptures that talked about drawing near to God, begging Him to help me. Sadly, I couldn't comprehend verses like James 4:8 that said, "Draw near to God and He will draw near to you" (NASB). I felt like something was wrong with me because I didn't feel close to Him.

JOY IN THE JOURNEY

I have always believed that there was a very real person behind the words on the pages of Scripture but have been afraid to trust God completely. It wasn't until I opened my sealed box of pain and looked intently at the truth inside that things began to change. Acknowledging the truth of my past was the first step toward healing. It awakened a deep longing within me to know and be known by my heavenly Father. I was now ready to move beyond theology and experience a true encounter with Jesus.

In order to feel safe with God and step toward an intimate relationship, I had to set out on the toughest spiritual journey I've ever been on. This meant that I had to break down my protective wall and search diligently for Him like I'd never searched for anything in my life. A priceless treasure waited for me in the end. I was thrilled when I finally experienced the comfort I had been longing for in the embrace of the Holy One. I have found healing, wholeness, and deliverance in God's presence.

As I ache with those of you whose hearts have been broken, I wish I could put my arms around you and whisper, "Shh. Shh. It's okay. You are loved." There is One who can help you return to joy, and He is very near. The Holy One loves you more than you can imagine and desires for you to begin walking the broken road so that you can find comfort in His loving embrace.

> You will make known to me the path of life;
> In Your presence is fullness of joy;
> In Your right hand there are pleasures forever.
> PSALM 16:11, NASB

WHY THIS JOURNEY?
STUDY

DAY 1: THE JOURNEY

1. Read Psalm 16:11. Personalize it here by restating it in your own words. Make it about God and you personally.

2. Think back to a time in your childhood when you were wounded. Was there someone to help you return to joy? Describe what happened and how you felt. What happened if there was no one to do this for you?

3. Read John 15:11 and describe what God desires for you.

4. Think about your present life. How would you describe your joy tank? Is it full, empty, or somewhere in between? Explain your answer.

5. If you had been granted one wish as a child, what would you have chosen and why?

6. What would you choose if you were granted one wish today? Why?

7. Read Deuteronomy 11:18-23. Describe how your family practiced or ignored these spiritual life lessons.

8. How has this affected you personally?

9. Make a list of the baggage you carried into your relationship with Christ and ask God to show you where it originated. Record your thoughts here.

10. What do Psalm 25:4 and Proverbs 20:24 say about the journey toward healing?

DAY 2: JOY STOLEN

1. Read John 10:10 and write it in your own words so that a child can understand what it means.

2. Are you experiencing the abundant life that Christ offers—or the devastating results of the evil one? Explain your answer.

3. What has Satan taken or tried to steal from you? What methods has he used to do this?

4. Has your joy been stolen? What does John 16:22 say about this?

5. Can you identify with any of the lies listed on pages 6–7? List the ones you have been tempted to believe.

6. Think back to the time when each of these lies first seemed true in your life. What was the source of this lie? (Explain what happened to make you believe the lie.)

7. Use three words to describe how these lies make you feel.

8. What did God promise in Isaiah 28:16? Who is this cornerstone?

9. What do you want your foundation to be: God's truth or lies from Satan? Explain your answer.

DAY 3: AVOIDING THE JOURNEY

1. Can you identify with any of the methods of coping with pain listed in this chapter? Explain your answer.

2. Are there any other ways that you have dealt with your pain? Describe what happened. (Coping mechanisms can be things like entertainment, work, church activities, relationships, sex, vacations, and projects.)

3. Spend some time reflecting on Psalm 116:1-2 and ask God to help you believe that He loves you in this way.

4. Read Psalm 51:6 and 1 Corinthians 16:13 in the New Living Translation. Use these verses to write an explanation that a child could understand about the importance of living a life of truth.

DAY 4: STARTING THE JOURNEY

1. Have you lived a life of truth, or have you worn a mask instead? Explain why you made this choice. What was the result?

2. How do you feel about taking off your mask? Describe your feelings here.

3. Jesus cautioned the Jewish leaders about the dangers of pursuing knowledge about God instead of a relationship with Him. Read John 5:39-40 and describe the warning that He gave.

4. Are you reading the Word of God but afraid to seek the God of the Word? Be honest and describe your answer here.

5. In light of this chapter, how can you personally apply Ephesians 4:25 and 1 John 2:21?

6. If you attempt to keep your pain stuffed down by living behind a mask, it will eventually bubble up. Have you experienced any physical, emotional, or spiritual problems as a result of this? Describe what happened.

DAY 5: JOY IN THE JOURNEY

1. Read Jeremiah 31:3, John 12:32, and James 4:8a. What do these verses tell you about drawing near to God?

2. What is your honest reaction to this truth?

3. Are you satisfied with where you are in your relationship with the Holy One? If not, how would you like for it to change?

4. Read Deuteronomy 4:29 and 10:12-13. Use these verses to explain how to "find God" so that a child can understand.

5. Walking the broken road to intimacy is not an easy journey. Are you willing to make a commitment to push through the pain so that you experience God's comfort? Explain your answer here.

6. Write a prayer telling the Holy One how you feel about this and ask Him to help you. Remember that you can be honest with Him because He knows your heart and loves you just as you are.

7. Spend time before the Lord, reflecting on Psalm 106:44-45. Record your thoughts here or in a journal.

CHAPTER 2

THE VALLEY OF WEEPING

Suffering for beauty is a concept familiar to most women. We starve ourselves to look good for a special event, pluck or wax hair from various places on our bodies, squeeze our feet into uncomfortable high heels, undergo acid or chemical peels, or even have surgery to enhance a part of our anatomy. For millions of Chinese women, this quest went even further—their feet were bound to turn them into the prized "three-inch golden lotuses." I recently read the heartbreaking novel called *Snow Flower and the Secret Fan*. It is a story about Lily, a Chinese girl who was forced to go through the ancient custom of foot-binding. This was an excruciating process where her feet were bound tightly to prevent further growth. Like many little girls, Lily endured this horrific procedure in hopes of attaining the smallest feet in her province. Lily's mother's words reminded me of my healing journey: "Only through pain will you have beauty. Only through suffering will you find peace."[1]

Trauma comes into our lives in all shapes and sizes. Suffering often festers deep inside our hearts, slowly stealing our peace, faith, and health a little bit at a time. So often we carefully build walls to protect our hearts. When we finally come to the end of ourselves and our fortresses begin to crumble, we have a choice to make. We can wallow in our pain or try to push it down again, or we can step onto the broken road, even though we aren't sure where the path is leading.

GRIEVING IN THE VALLEY

No one likes pain, so we do everything in our power to avoid going there. It's only when we embrace our brokenness that we can step forward into God's healing—even if it means stepping out on a broken road.

Walking the broken road to intimacy is a hard journey that will lead us to different places, but getting started is always extremely difficult. And where do we start? In the Valley of Weeping where, like Lily, we experience excruciating pain. Psalm 84:6 talks about this place of grieving: "When they walk through the Valley of Weeping, it will become a place of refreshing springs. The autumn rains will clothe it with blessings."

At the beginning of my journey, I longed to swim in those refreshing springs, but I was weighed down. The baggage I had brought into my relationship with Christ and the baggage that was added afterward kept me from experiencing the joy that God desired for me.

Have you ever had to repack your suitcase at the airport because it was over the weight limit? In the same way, we sometimes take unnecessary things on our healing journey. The first thing we have to do is to sort through our baggage and get rid of the things that are causing problems. This is not easy—it means we have to open up each wound and remember the hurtful things that caused it.

OUR BAGGAGE

The relationships and circumstances we've experienced in childhood can shape us in profound ways. Whether we want to put our parents on a pedestal or get as far away from them as possible, their words and actions impact who we are today. Broken relationships with anyone from whom we longed for approval and love, personal losses, decisions we've made, and circumstances we've been thrust into can cause us to carry various types of baggage into our adulthood. Emotional baggage can stem from two types of past trauma—neglect and abuse—as well as from mistakes and present losses.

Neglect

Neglect is caused by the absence of good things we should all receive to provide emotional stability. This kind of trauma occurs when a child is not cherished and understood. This includes lack of nonsexual physical affection, age-inappropriate limitations and expectations, and physical deprivations of food, shelter, clothing, and medical care. The painful feelings that result from neglect can have a negative effect on future relationships.

Many people consider neglect insignificant and find it hard to recognize as the cause of their depression, fear, and isolation. They end up feeling confused about why they have negative self-esteem, why they are afraid to trust others, and why they struggle with perfectionism. This baggage must be dealt with before trust can be restored. This involves recognizing the injury, grieving the loss, receiving life-giving truth, and developing an intimate relationship with a few safe people and the only One who can fill the gaps formed by neglect.

Abuse

The second type of trauma is caused by abuse. Childhood abuse includes being abandoned by a parent or guardian; being hurt by bullies and mean girls; experiencing physical, emotional, or sexual abuse; and witnessing abuse done to others.

When intense trauma occurs to a child, memories can be stored in the recesses of his or her mind. Amnesia, or dissociation, is an automatic brain function where a person instantly forgets something that is too overwhelming to deal with. The memory is sometimes stored in the brain, so it can be remembered at a later time. At other times no memory at all is stored, and the past remains a blur. This is God's gift to help the victim survive without losing their mind. Though dissociation itself is evidence that abuse occurred, sometimes harrowing memories need to be brought out in a safe environment so that fear and other negative responses can be deactivated. This needs to be done under the supervision of a professional counselor who is trained in this area.

Far too many also experience emotional, physical, and sexual abuse in adolescence and adulthood. As I have shared my story with others, my greatest surprise has been the number of women who have told me they were sexually assaulted by someone they know. Most of them feel responsible in some way because they didn't scream for help or report the incident for what it was: sexual assault. According to the US Department of Justice, four out of five rapes are committed by someone known to the victim[2] and 68 percent of sexual assaults are not reported to the police.[3] Sadly, the victims carry great shame.

Any kind of past traumatic experience can cause the brain's control center to be altered, resulting in post-traumatic stress disorder (PTSD). When this happens the person can experience flashbacks; intrusive thoughts and memories; hyperactivity; jumpiness; avoidance of people, places, and things; and many other symptoms. The effects will vary and can be debilitating, depending on how often the traumatic event occurred and how long it went on.

PRESENT LOSSES

Past trauma is not always the cause of present burdens. Present losses such as rejection, illness, the loss of a spouse or loved one, and even the loss of a dream can be just as damaging as trauma suffered in childhood. Nothing that steals your joy is insignificant. If it is not dealt with, it can create harmful baggage that causes negative emotions.

Sherry experienced deep grief when her husband died suddenly. Here is her story:

> My world has been turned upside down without warning.
> I feel like I can't eat, sleep, or even breathe. With tears
> streaming down my face I ask: Why did this happen?
> Why not take me? What about the future? What about
> the young tender hearts that do not understand? How can
> I go on?
>   I can place one foot in front of the other even if I don't
> know where I'm going. I will remember that He is God
> and I am not. I will cling to Him for love, protection, and
> counsel, no matter what storm comes. He has done great
> things for me and He will continue to do great things.
> With this knowledge my tears are being replaced with a
> deeper understanding of who He truly is . . . who He has
> always been—the great I Am.

Sherry found comfort in the Valley of Weeping. She recognized that even though she felt confused and off balance, the Holy One was with her, gently guiding her every step.

MISTAKES

The baggage of present and past mistakes can be as damaging as neglect and abuse. Burying sinful things we did in the past or are presently involved in perpetuates harmful lies, shame, and guilt.

When the apostle Paul was brought before King Agrippa in Acts 26, he admitted that he had been a zealous persecutor of the church, abusing Christians before he came to know Christ. He had a clear understanding of his sinful past and didn't try to keep it hidden from others. He was able to put this baggage behind him by confessing it and moving forward into the powerful ministry that God called him to.

You may be thinking, *Paul did those horrible things before he was a Christian. My sin is greater because I've made a lot of mistakes since I accepted Christ as my Savior.* We are declared righteous before God when we receive Christ, but we still struggle with temptations because we live in a fallen world. As Paul said,

> I know that good itself does not dwell in me, that is,
> in my sinful nature. For I have the desire to do what is
> good, but I cannot carry it out. For I do not do the good
> I want to do, but the evil I do not want to do—this I
> keep on doing. Now if I do what I do not want to do,
> it is no longer I who do it, but it is sin living in me that
> does it. ROMANS 7:18-20, NIV

All of us have made mistakes both before and after we began our journey with Christ. When we ignore them and try to pretend that these sinful choices didn't happen, we are left with heavy baggage that weighs us down and keeps us from moving forward. Unloading this weight by bringing that which is in the darkness into the light is freeing. We are new creatures saved by grace. With His nail-scarred hands of mercy, Jesus will lead us on the pathway where we can find healing.

Like many people, I lived a life of duplicity, trying to hide my true self from others. I believed that people would not like me if they knew what had been done to me and what I had done in response, so I hid it in the darkness. While in the Valley of Weeping, I cried tears for the bad things done to me and for the bad things I did as a result. It was horrifying and humbling to admit the things I had done in secret. But I knew that the only way healing could come was if I bowed all of my pain before the Holy One and allowed Him to heal me from the inside out (James 4:9).

Recognizing harmful baggage and disposing of it is difficult, but it cannot be ignored. Inner healing is God's work, but we must confess and confront our weaknesses and wounds, even though it is painful. He is the only One who can put your broken heart and fractured soul back together the way it was intended to be.

REMOVING ROADBLOCKS

Unfortunately, there are many roadblocks that keep us from eliminating heavy baggage. The most obvious one is the roadblock of *fear*. It is human nature to protect our hearts from anything that hurts, so we end up suppressing painful memories. In the midst of my pain, I felt that I needed to be strong and independent. The emotions that accompanied the pain made me feel weak and fearful, so I avoided them at all costs. I was afraid that I would never be able to stop crying, so it took a huge leap of faith to step into the Valley of Weeping.

Joy, a precious young woman who experienced indescribable childhood trauma, writes about this:

> Life is good, but the painful memories from the past are seeping into my present and I am grieving. It is good to cry—better than not being able to, but I hate that it is obvious to the people around me. It makes me feel guilty, like I am doing something terribly wrong which causes more pain and grief. I don't like being known as the girl who is grieving or as a person who is broken, but

my grief seems unbearable. I don't understand why the Lord has me engulfed in sorrow so I cry out for Him to remove this bitter cup.

Some people do not understand the importance of grieving, so they teach their children that crying is wrong. This is another roadblock to grieving: the roadblock of *misunderstanding*. My mother made me feel ashamed if I cried when I was wounded and taught me that I should never allow anyone to know that I was weak. As a result, I learned to hide my tears at a young age. When I heard Mom admonish my six-year-old nephew (her grandson) to stop crying at the funeral of a close relative, I realized why grieving was hard for me. So I wrapped my arms around my nephew and gave him permission to cry as much as he wanted to.

Some Christians stumble on this roadblock because they believe that grieving is sinful. They argue that mourning losses requires putting too much focus on self, using Philippians 3:13-14 as justification: "Brothers and sisters, I do not consider myself yet to have taken hold of it. But one thing I do: Forgetting what is behind and straining toward what is ahead, I press on toward the goal to win the prize for which God has called me heavenward in Christ Jesus" (NIV).

But when you look at these verses in context, it's clear that Paul's concern was not about putting painful things in the past. Instead, he wanted to put behind him everything he had achieved by his own power, recognizing harmful beliefs and actions that needed to change and replacing them with the truth. He had a clear understanding of his unhealthy baggage and what he needed to do to get rid of it:

Yes, everything else is worthless when compared with the infinite value of knowing Christ Jesus my Lord. For his sake I have discarded everything else, counting it all

as garbage, so that I could gain Christ and become one
with him.   PHILIPPIANS 3:8-9

Like Paul, we too need to resolve our wounds in order to put
them in the past and move forward. An emotional wound can
be like a festering abscess deeply embedded beneath the skin's
surface. The healing process must take place from the inside out
so that all of the painful infection can be taken care of. In the
same way, emotional healing can occur only when we invite God
to heal our wounds from the inside out.

GOD IS "WITH ME"

God is not here to take away our pain, but to fill it up with
His presence. We are reminded throughout the Old and New
Testaments that the presence of the Holy One is our firm foun-
dation when our world is shaken (Psalm 16:8).

The two simple words *with me* encompass more weight than
we can fathom. The disciples were in serious trouble one evening
as they battled against the stormy sea. I'm sure they were afraid, but
their fear turned into terror when they saw a figure walking toward
them on the water. "But Jesus spoke to them at once. 'Don't be
afraid,' he said. 'Take courage. I am here!'" (Matthew 14:27). The
very presence of the Holy One may not change our circumstances,
but it can change the way we view them.

To think that the all-powerful God of the universe is always
with me changes the way I view everything. We live in a broken
world, but because God is with us we can have joy, even when
things are hard. This is what the apostle Paul meant when he
wrote, "Our hearts ache, but we always have joy. We are poor, but
we give spiritual riches to others. We own nothing, and yet we have
everything" (2 Corinthians 6:10). We have everything we need
when God is with us.

Weeping can be a beautiful form of worship when we humble

ourselves before the Holy One and bow our pain before His feet. When I do this, I don't presume that God is going to change my painful situation, but I am reminded that He is with me each step of the way, and I find hope in the midst of the storm.

THE BEAUTY OF BROKENNESS

There is an old Jewish proverb that says, "What soap is to the body, tears are for the soul." God uses tears to cleanse the spiritual and emotional part of us. When I first began to grieve, my tears were frozen and I didn't know how to thaw them out. I finally gave myself permission to grieve when I understood the beauty of brokenness and realized that my tears are important to God.

Emotional tears are different from the tears produced by physical irritants. Scientists have discovered that there is a protein released from the body through emotional tears that actually helps reduce the person's stress response. In other words, our heavenly Father created us so that having a good, long cry can produce a physiological response that can make us feel better. When we stop fighting and embrace our brokenness, crying out to the only One who can heal us, we can finally experience the nearness of our Beloved (Psalm 34:18).

Pain comes in all colors. Mine came through abandonment and abuse. Elaine's came through what felt like abandonment disguised as an army assignment:

> I HAAAAAAAAAAATE THIS!!! My husband is deployed, the dog is sick, the kids are a mess, and I'm worried about my sick mother and angry at my father who isn't taking responsibility for her. I feel a tight knot in my throat and stomach; I can't eat or sleep. And on top of everything, a stomach bug decided to grace our home this week and left us all heaving over the toilet. At midnight on Christmas Eve the hot water pipe burst under the sink. I finally

collapsed onto my bed, sobbing. *I just need someone to hold me while I cry. Why, God, why????* And then I heard a soft whisper: "I love you, Elaine."

In that moment I knew that my tears mattered. In the midst of my utter desperation, the Lord shouted into my pain . . . and the atmosphere changed. God's very presence came into my sanctuary, and in the silence He whispered to my heart, "Elaine, I rejoice over you! Do you not see? Do you not understand? I have loved you with an everlasting love, and you will be called Sought After, the City No Longer Deserted" (Isaiah 62:5, 12; Jeremiah 31:3, NIV).

He has lifted me from the dust on the floor to His shining face and I respond, "For as long as it takes, beautiful Jesus. Thank You."

Sorrow is an emotion that needs to be expressed. Sometimes we grieve with hope, softly crying on our knees before the Lord, believing that He will rescue us. At other times we grieve without hope, thinking that we are far too broken for Him to fix. In the midst of my grief, there were times when I was in so much pain that I found myself stomping up and down our staircase, begging God to heal me. I had to use a washcloth to wipe my tears at times because a tissue was insufficient. Sometimes all I could do was scream into a pillow. There were also a few gut-wrenching moments when I found myself on the floor of our bathroom with my face in the toilet. On many days I felt like I would never get to the end of my grief.

I am comforted knowing that Jesus also visited the Valley of Weeping: "While Jesus was here on earth, he offered prayers and pleadings, with a loud cry and tears, to the one who could rescue him from death. And God heard his prayers because of his deep reverence for God" (Hebrews 5:7).

Jesus cried out loudly to God, offering sweet tears of surrender.

His brokenness was never more evident than when He humbled Himself and sweetly surrendered to the Father's plan, even though it meant suffering and death. Recognizing that Jesus went before me infused me with hope. He paved the way so that I could have courage in the midst of my pain.

Tears are the language of the soul, and God can use them to bring us to a point of surrender. When we finally give up control and allow tears of sorrow to fall, healing can be the result. In fact, one of the Hebrew words for grieving actually means "to shape." This verb beautifully describes God's redemptive work in the midst of our tears. As a potter uses water to soften clay, the Holy One uses our tears to soften our hard hearts until they beat in time with His. Therefore, our tears, both happy and sad, are the precious offering of a surrendered heart when poured out at the feet of our Beloved (Luke 7:38).

The Valley of Weeping became a holy place for me. No human words can describe what took place during my time there. I learned that it is sweet to be broken, battered, and incapable of doing anything without the Holy One. For the first time in my life, I began to see that it was okay to surrender my will to my Beloved and become desperately weak and needy. God created all of us with relational needs and is pleased when we admit that we are totally inadequate without Him. It is only when we are weak and needy that His glory can break forth with divine power and might in our lives.

The Valley of Weeping is a bittersweet place where we realize that we are helpless but not hopeless. Our God is with us in our pain and can give divine comfort every step of the journey . . . if we allow Him to. He is lifting our downcast faces to behold His glory and bringing redemption from our stories.

I will never forget this awful time,
    as I grieve over my loss.

Yet I still dare to hope
> when I remember this:

The faithful love of the LORD never ends!
> His mercies never cease.
Great is his faithfulness;
> his mercies begin afresh each morning.
I say to myself, "The LORD is my inheritance;
> therefore, I will hope in him!"

LAMENTATIONS 3:20-24

THE VALLEY OF WEEPING STUDY

DAY 1: GRIEVING IN THE VALLEY

1. What does the Bible say about grieving in Psalm 6:6 and Psalm 31:7-9? How is sadness expressed?

2. What did Jesus say about grieving in Matthew 5:4?

3. Is this what you were taught as a child? Explain your answer.

4. Was there any neglect involved in your childhood? (Remember that neglect is the absence of good things we should all receive to provide emotional stability.) Can you identify any baggage (negative emotions) connected to this? Explain your answer.

5. Have you been tempted to minimize, spiritualize, or deny anything that may have resulted from neglect? Explain why. What was the result?

6. Did you experience any emotional, physical, or sexual abuse in your past? Describe what happened.

7. Can you identify any baggage (negative emotions) connected to this abuse? Explain your answer.

8. Have you been tempted to minimize, spiritualize, or deny anything that may have resulted from this? Explain why. What was the result?

9. Read 1 Peter 5:6-7 and reflect on these verses. Take some time to cast your pain before the Holy One. Allow yourself to feel any sad or negative emotions resulting from neglect and/or abuse. Ask the Holy One to show you if there are any lies or other baggage connected to it. Remember that you are not alone as you do this. Record your thoughts here or in a journal.

DAY 2: OUR BAGGAGE: LOSSES

1. Have you experienced a recent loss or disappointment that is causing you to struggle with negative emotions? Describe your feelings here.

2. Can you identify any baggage (negative emotions) connected to this loss? List the baggage here.

3. Have you been tempted to minimize, spiritualize, or deny anything that may have resulted from this disappointment? Explain why. What was the result?

4. Describe what the psalmist did in Psalm 42 when he was downcast in spirit. What can you learn from this?

5. How did Jesus respond in Luke 7:11-13 when he came upon the widow from Nain whose son had died?

6. Do you believe that He feels the same for you when you are hurting? Why or why not?

7. God may not choose to take away your pain, but He promises something just as amazing. Read Psalm 68:19 and describe what it is. How does this change the way you view your trials?

8. Take some time to lay your pain before the Holy One. Allow yourself to feel any type of emotions resulting from your present losses. Ask the Holy One to show you if there

are any lies or other baggage connected to it. Remember that the Holy One is with you. Record your thoughts.

DAY 3: OUR BAGGAGE: MISTAKES

1. Read Psalm 51:1-7. Have you, like David, done something shameful in the past and kept it hidden in the dark? If so, what impact has this had on you? Can you identify any baggage (negative emotions) connected to this past sin? List it here.

2. Have you been tempted to minimize, spiritualize, or deny anything that may have resulted from this sinful action? Explain your answer. Take some time to lay this before the Holy One and ask Him to reveal any lies or other baggage connected to it. Record your thoughts.

3. Are you ready to confess any hidden sin? Explain what happens when you do. Remember 1 John 1:9: "If we confess our sins to him, he can be depended on to forgive us and to cleanse us from every wrong" (TLB). Record your thoughts.

4. Can you identify with any of the roadblocks that keep people from grieving listed on pages 25–26? List them here and explain the effect they have had on you.

5. When trials come along we sometimes feel like God has abandoned us. What does Psalm 43:2-5 encourage you to do when this happens? How can you apply these verses when you are grieving?

6. Are there any other roadblocks that are keeping you from grieving your pain? Explain your answer.

DAY 4: GOD IS "WITH ME"

1. How do you feel about the statement on page 27: "God is not here to take away our pain, but to fill it up with His presence"? (You can be honest).

2. What is the offer of hope in the midst of trials given in Deuteronomy 31:8, Jeremiah 1:8, and John 14:17?

3. Write a paragraph about a trial you are facing (or have faced in the past) with Mark 6:47-50 in mind. Add the last part of verse 50 to your paragraph: "But Jesus spoke to them at once. 'Don't be afraid,' he said. 'Take courage! I am here.'" How does this change the way you feel about your trial?

4. How does the thought of God being with you in your trials change the way you view your healing journey?

5. What happens when the things in the darkness are exposed to God's light according to Psalm 139:12 and Luke 11:36?

6. It is important to bring everything into the light so that we can be healed. Is there anything in your life that is still hidden in the darkness? Spend some time in prayer, asking the Holy One to reveal this to you.

DAY 5: THE BEAUTY OF BROKENNESS

1. Jesus went to Bethany when He heard about Lazarus's death. Read John 11:31-35 and explain how He responded to Mary's grief.

2. What does this say about Jesus' heart for those who are grieving? Do you believe that He cares about your grief in this same way? Why or why not?

3. Read Psalm 51:16-17 and write it so that a child can understand it. What emotion is evoked when you consider this truth?

4. Jesus paved the way through the Valley of Weeping for us. Read 1 Peter 4:12-13. What should our response to the healing journey be in light of these verses?

CHAPTER 3

THE GATEWAY OF HOPE

SOMETIMES, in the midst of the Valley of Weeping, we feel as if there's no way out. As I journeyed through it, I felt helpless and hopeless one minute and hopeful that I would survive the next. After countless tears and what seemed like an eternity, I felt stuck in my grief. That's when the Holy One led me to the Gateway of Hope, where I learned how to bow my pain in worship and find comfort in His presence. I was finally able to return to joy. This may sound easy, but be forewarned . . . it was no simple task.

In Hosea 2, God compared His chosen bride, Israel, to a prostitute who worshiped foreign gods. The Father longed for His precious wife to come back to the safety of His presence, but Israel was stuck in a cycle of self-destruction and could not find the way out. The Holy One offered an unbelievable solution to her misery:

"But then I will win her back once again.
  I will lead her into the desert
  and speak tenderly to her there.

I will return her vineyards to her
    and transform the Valley of Trouble into
        a gateway of hope.
She will give herself to me there,
    as she did long ago when she was young,
    when I freed her from her captivity in Egypt.
When that day comes," says the LORD,
    "you will call me 'my husband'
    instead of 'my master.'
O Israel, I will wipe the many names of Baal
        from your lips,
    and you will never mention them again.
On that day I will make a covenant
    with all the wild animals and the birds of the sky
and the animals that scurry along the ground
    so they will not harm you.
I will remove all weapons of war from the land,
    all swords and bows,
so you can live unafraid
    in peace and safety.
I will make you my wife forever,
    showing you righteousness and justice,
        unfailing love and compassion.
I will be faithful to you and make you mine,
    and you will finally know me as the LORD."

HOSEA 2:14-20

The restoration of the marriage between the Lord and Israel was described in terms of a betrothal much more binding than our contemporary marriage engagements. At that time, the law treated a betrothed couple as though they were legally married, but Israel was a runaway bride who ended up in deep trouble. The Gateway of Hope would lead her out of the Valley of Trouble and back to her husband, who loved her even though she had been unfaithful. However, this time it would be a completely different relationship. She would no longer relate to Him as Master in a formal relationship. This gateway would bring her to a deeper level of intimacy, where she would know Him as her beloved husband and her Lord.

Likewise, the Holy One desires for each of us to step through the Gateway of Hope into His presence, where we can exchange a polite relationship with our Maker for something far more captivating. He longs for us to find comfort in an intimate relationship where there is healing and restoration for all that has been lost. This is the gateway that leads to true joy.

THE CALL TO WORSHIP

And what is the Gateway of Hope? Worship—because worship is the bridge between heaven and earth. Paul taught the believers in Ephesus, "Because of Christ and our faith in him, we can now come boldly and confidently into God's presence" (Ephesians 3:12). As we go boldly into His throne room in worship, we begin to experience face-to-face intimacy with our Beloved.

Several years ago at our annual women's retreat my friend Linda Dillow challenged us to commit to worshiping God twenty minutes each day for one month. She explained that worship is different from prayers of petition, where we ask God to do something for us or for someone else. It is also different from prayers of thanksgiving, where we focus on what He has done in the past. In worship, we simply adore God by focusing on who He truly is. These words from A. P. Gibbs helped me understand this more clearly: "In prayer we are occupied with our needs, in thanksgiving we are occupied with our blessings, but in worship we are totally occupied with God Himself."[1]

To worship is to attribute worth to God through obedience to His Word as well as through offering praise for who He is.

It is multifaceted and can be as simple as singing a love song to Him. In this place of worship, we no longer focus on our circumstances, but on the only One who can carry us in the midst of the storm, no matter how tumultuous. But if we're honest, worship is the last thing we feel like doing when we are in pain.

I have heard it said that worship begins with a broken heart. I certainly had a broken heart, but I was afraid of the unknown. *What does worship look like? Will I have to fully surrender and give up control of my life? Can I trust that God will show up?* I was desperate and didn't know where to turn, so I decided to take Linda's worship challenge. Even though it was extremely hard at first, I began to meet with God in worship each day.

Praying only words of praise and blessing to the Lord without giving any requests seemed impossible. I ran out of things to say after five minutes and wondered what in the world I would do with the rest of my time. Amazingly, as I continued to press into the Holy One, those twenty minutes became thirty and sometimes even extended to an hour. Before long I could hardly pull myself away from this glorious place where I found the heart of God.

We can diligently study the Word of God, but not until we begin to passionately seek the God of the Word will we find true comfort from the Holy One. As we bow our pain in worship, the pieces of our broken hearts will finally be emptied at His feet—and He will gather them up and gently put our hearts back together again.

WHAT DOES WORSHIP LOOK LIKE?

I used to think that worship was the first twenty minutes of a Sunday morning church service when songs are sung to the Lord. But it is far more than that. The Bible clearly reveals that praise and worship are the primary vehicles for entering into communion with God. This can be done corporately, as believers gather together to ascribe to God the glory He deserves, and it can also be a personal experience. Both are important, but sometimes we are confused about individual worship, which involves both the posture of our hearts and the use of our spiritual senses.

WORSHIP IN SPIRIT AND TRUTH

Many of the words for worship in the Old Testament pertain to body posture—kneeling, bowing, prostrating oneself, singing songs, offering sacrifices, lifting up hands, etc. The main Hebrew word for worship literally means to "bow down, prostrate oneself, before a monarch or superior, in homage."[2] We are all created individually by God and have our own unique worship preferences. Some people worship with uninhibited expression while others are uncomfortable with any type of external response.

My friend Deborah has taught me much about what worship looks like. A few months after Deborah graduated from high school, her family was involved in a tragic car accident that took her father's life and left her mother permanently disabled. Even after this tragedy, Deborah learned to worship on her knees from her godly mother's example:

> After several surgeries and months convalescing, Mother
> faced the challenges in life with unwavering faith in
> our Lord. Although one of her knees and both legs
> were badly injured from the accident, for the rest of
> her life she painfully got down on them to kneel when
> she worshiped. She told me that her pain was nothing
> compared to the pain that Jesus endured. Her strength
> came from a deep and abiding love for our Savior that
> was stronger than any adversity she faced.

God is pleased when we worship with extravagant, demonstrative, passionate praise, but sincere worship is more than body language. Jesus taught that worship is the language of the heart. In the discussion between Jesus and the woman at the well, our Lord described what true worship looks like: "But the time is coming—indeed it's here now—when true worshipers will worship the Father in spirit and in truth. The Father is looking for those who will worship him that way. For God is Spirit, so those who worship him must worship in spirit and in truth" (John 4:23-24).

God is the sovereign King who created the whole universe. He doesn't need anything from us, yet these verses reveal that He seeks men and women who will worship Him with unwavering devotion. To worship in spirit and truth means that we must remove any mask in order to be real and completely honest before God. We hide sinful behavior and shameful thoughts because we think doing so will keep us safe, but in fact, it is the death of intimacy. When we lay our shame before our Beloved and bask in His forgiveness, a stronghold is broken and we can live with great joy (Romans 4:7-8).

One of the Greek words for worship in the New Testament literally means "to kiss the hand to (towards) one."[3] When I blow kisses to my grandchildren, my heart is spilling over with love for them. In a similar way, all walls come tumbling down when I allow my heart to be filled with overflowing passion for my Beloved in worship. This is worshiping in spirit and truth.

SPIRITUAL SENSES

When the Lord brought the children of Israel out of Egypt, He spoke to them with an audible voice. We may no longer experience God in this way, but we have something that is just as spectacular: "Ears to hear and eyes to see—both are gifts from the LORD" (Proverbs 20:12).

We live in a world with two dimensions. We are born into the physical world with five physical senses. We can see, hear, feel, smell, and taste temporal things. But the Bible teaches about another kind of birth for those who believe in Christ: "They are reborn—not with a physical birth resulting from human passion or plan, but a birth that comes from God" (John 1:13). This means that we are born into the physical world and then reborn into the Kingdom of God if we accept Christ as our Savior. When this occurs, we receive spiritual senses that enable us to perceive the eternal things of the spiritual world (2 Corinthians 4:18). Although these spiritual senses are harder to discern, they are just as real as our five physical senses.

We can only use our spiritual senses when we surrender our wills and allow the Holy Spirit to fill us with His divine presence. As Linda Dillow states, "In worship, my spirit flows to His and His Spirit back to mine."[4] This is a beautiful picture of being one with the Lord (1 Corinthians 2:10-12).

Eternity is the spiritual dimension of the invisible God where we exercise our spiritual senses. Because these mysterious senses aren't natural to us, it takes faith to use them. When we step out in faith, however, we are able to supernaturally experience the unseen things of the heavenly world (Hebrews 11:1). We participate in heavenly activity when our praises join with the angels and saints who are worshiping God in heaven (Deuteronomy 32:43). When we use our spiritual senses, we can see with His eyes, hear with His ears, touch others with His hands, taste the sweetness of His Word and presence, and have a tender heart like Jesus.

WRESTLING WITH GOD

Surrendering our hearts in worship is no easy thing. When I first took the worship challenge, I mostly wrestled with God for control. I asked honest questions like *Where were You when those bad things happened to me? Why didn't You protect me? If I couldn't trust You then, why should I trust You now?* I was trying my hardest to press into the Lord, but I couldn't get past the hard questions.

I knew that I could learn from King David, who was desperate for an encounter with God, so I turned to the Psalms for direction. I found that David often wrestled with the Lord:

> Have mercy on me, O God, have mercy!
>   I look to you for protection.
> I will hide beneath the shadow of your wings
>   until the danger passes by.
> I cry out to God Most High,
>   to God who will fulfill his purpose for me.
>
> PSALM 57:1-2

David cried out to God in his pain, and I recognized that I needed to do the same, but that felt extremely risky. I knew that God could answer my cry for help, but I wasn't sure that He would.

Some people will say that it is sinful to question God or be angry with Him. But it's okay to be honest with Him, even if we're mad, as long as we don't stay there. Psalm 139 tells us that God already knows our thoughts, so we don't need to bury them or pretend that they aren't there (verses 1-2). Anger, fear, and confusion are natural responses to the sometimes harsh world we live in. When the disciples' faith was shaken because their boat was being tossed by a fierce storm, they woke Jesus up with this question: "Teacher, don't you care that we're going to drown?" (Mark 4:38). They had worked, played, eaten, and traveled with Jesus. They knew Him as well as anyone on earth could—and they weren't afraid to be honest with Him.

God is big enough to deal with your hard questions. Only when we bring all of our negative emotions out of the darkness and into the light can we see the truth. That is why we need to be sincere about our feelings and deal with them in a healthy way. When we find God's presence in worship, we are able to

hear with our spiritual ears and find the answers to our hard
questions. And even if we don't find the answers, the questions
no longer haunt us when we are safe in His warm embrace.

My sweet friend Angie struggled with hard questions when
her daughter was tragically killed in an accident:

> During a family gathering, Mallory, our precious five-
> year-old daughter, died in an ATV accident. To say that
> my world was turned upside down is an understatement.
> Words can't begin to describe how I felt. The pain
> was raw, complicated, and confusing. I had so many
> questions, so many emotions. *What do I do now? How
> will I survive? How will my other children handle this?
> Where is God? Why didn't He intervene?*
>
> Something miraculously changed the day of Mallory's
> funeral, a day I didn't think I could live through. As
> our family walked into the sanctuary, we were met
> with praise songs. Suddenly I began to worship, and I
> experienced a peace that I had never experienced before.
> I was able to praise our Father, knowing that Mallory
> was also worshiping Him in her forever home.
>
> My emotions have ebbed and flowed as days have
> turned into weeks, weeks into months, and months
> into years. I had always believed that God loved me and
> wanted the best for me, but losing Mallory caused me
> to wrestle. I wasn't finished being her mom and couldn't
> understand why He allowed the accident to happen. In
> the midst of all the questions, however, I never doubted
> that Mallory was safe with Jesus.
>
> God has revealed so many things to me about who
> He really is since then. I know without a doubt that I
> can trust Him with all of my questions and fears. I miss
> Mallory beyond words—and I will until the day we are

reunited—but I am choosing to worship God in the midst of my pain.

We must be honest about our questions and bow them before the Holy One. Only when we learn to bow our pain in worship will we find comfort in the Father's embrace.

WHERE IS GOD WHEN BAD THINGS HAPPEN?
Psalm 57:3 says,

> He sends from heaven and saves me,
>   rebuking those who hotly pursue me—
>   God sends forth his love and his faithfulness. (NIV)

David saw that God was his protector when evil men pursued him. Likewise, as I met the Lord in worship He began to show me that He was the one who had kept me safe for all of those years.

I've had lots of people try to explain where God was when bad things happened to me. Some said He was in the room, weeping in the corner while I was being abused. That didn't bring comfort because that would mean that God is passive. Others argued that He was doing His best to protect me, but that the perpetrator wouldn't listen. Well, doing His best was not good enough for me. That would mean that He is impotent. I could never trust a God who is passive and weak. As I was on my knees in desperation one day, I heard Him speak into my heart. It wasn't an audible voice, but a miraculous Spirit-to-spirit encounter.

As I listened with spiritual ears, He revealed Himself as the God of angel armies in the heavenly battle that I can't see (Isaiah 51:15). He isn't passively and impotently standing by, observing our pain and doing nothing. God is actively engaged in heavenly warfare, and electrifying power fills heaven and earth as He wages war against the forces of evil on our behalf. The angelic forces of light fight under His command, protecting our souls from being lost forever in Satan's grasp. This victory means that while we may be tormented, we are not defeated. Even though human hands under Satan's control may hurt our bodies, our spiritual destiny is forever safe in God's strong right hand.

NESTLING INSTEAD OF WRESTLING

Psalm 57:7 is a beautiful softening of the heart:

> My heart, O God, is steadfast,
>   my heart is steadfast;
>   I will sing and make music. (NIV)

Wait a minute. Is this the same David who was crying out to God for mercy just a few verses before? What happened to change his attitude?

Worshiping God in the midst of his trials helped David remember how powerful God is. As he bowed his pain in worship, he found divine comfort in God's presence and joy that made his heart sing. As a result, he was able to nestle into the Holy One.

Worship is telling God who He is, not because He needs to know, but because we need to remind ourselves of His true character. When I began the worship challenge, I argued with God at first, but I would always end up praising Him for any attribute I could think of. In time, God gently revealed His true heart for me, and I began to nestle instead of wrestle.

I love these words from Katie, a beautiful woman who has learned to nestle in God in a profound way:

> Married to my prince, a dream come true. Stay-at-
> home mom, Bible study leader. Taking care of my
> body and home, going on exciting dates and wonderful
> trips, and enjoying intimacy with the love of my life.

Picture-perfect life, right? Yet I am not enough for my husband.

Nightmare! Husband involved in two affairs simultaneously. Aching heart, immense fear, desperation, exhaustion, failure, stinging pain, doctor's exam, AIDS testing, utter, utter humiliation. My prince, my lover . . . all trust is stolen away. Oh, the suffering in silence, a few close prayer warriors, hours on my knees in worship.

How could this be? Slowly I begin to dance in the rain. The Lord becomes my sunshine, and I find I am glorious in Him. My soul opens wide and the holes are filled with His tenderness. He draws me close and we walk hand in hand. I'm not alone. Childlike dependence increases, He becomes my Prince, my refuge, my joy . . . and the fear is lifted. God comes through and He is enough.

Katie chose to bow her pain in worship. Nestled into the Holy One, she found comfort and healing. He has exchanged her fears and disappointments for a supernatural joy that cannot be taken away.

If I hadn't stepped through the Gateway of Hope and found healing comfort from the Lord in worship, I would have continued in my Christian walk just as I was—saved, walking in the Spirit the best I could, knowing many blessings and being used by Him, and yet never really knowing Him intimately. But now, like David, I am personally experiencing the compassionate Lord of the universe in an exciting new way. I have an incredible, insatiable appetite that can only be satisfied by His alluring presence. He is not invisible and far away as I thought—He is as near as my beating heart.

Satan desires to use your pain as a barrier to keep you from trusting God and others. When you bow it to the Holy One in worship, He will use it as a magnet to draw you to His heart. It is my prayer that you will step through the Gateway of Hope, where you can experience divine comfort that will help you return to joy as you worship in His presence.

> I come to your altar, O Lord,
> singing a song of thanksgiving
>   and telling of all your wonders.
> I love your sanctuary, Lord,
>   the place where your glorious presence dwells.

PSALM 26:6-8

THE GATEWAY OF HOPE
STUDY

DAY 1: STEPPING THROUGH THE GATEWAY OF HOPE

1. Read Hosea 2:14-20 and rewrite it in a way that a child could understand.

2. How would you describe your relationship with the Lord?

3. Do you desire to move to a deeper level of intimacy with Him? If so, what do you need to do in order to get there?

4. To worship is to attribute worth to God through obedience to His Word as well as through offering praise for who He is. When you think of worship, what does it look like to you and why?

5. Read Psalm 27:8. The psalmist, David, was open to God's call to worship. Can you say the same about yourself? Why or why not? Is there something you need to change in your worship experience? Explain.

6. Step through the Gateway of Hope and spend twenty
   minutes (or as many as you can) in worship today. Record
   your thoughts here or in a journal. (Optional: Worship
   through Psalm 29. Go slowly through the psalm, reading
   it aloud and adding your own elaborations for each verse.
   What does each verse make you want to say to God? Read
   the psalm again and choose a verse to commit to memory.
   Copy it into your journal and repeat it aloud. You can also
   sing along with worship music or pray other psalms aloud.
   Try different body positions, such as kneeling or standing
   with arms raised.)

DAY 2: WHAT DOES WORSHIP LOOK LIKE?

1. In the Old Testament we see that many of the words for
   worship pertain to body posture. Read 2 Chronicles 20:18,
   Psalm 63:3-4, and Psalm 100:2. What do you see about
   worship from these verses? How does this make you feel
   and why?

2. Jesus had many discussions with the spiritual leaders of the
   day. Read Matthew 15:8-9. What did Jesus say about their
   worship? What do you think He meant by this?

3. Jesus said we should worship in spirit and truth (John
   4:24). This means that we must remove all masks in order
   to be real and completely honest with God. Read Mark
   4:22 and explain it in your own words.

4. What happens to the things we try to keep hidden in secret according to Luke 8:17?

5. Is there anything hidden in your life that needs to be brought into the light? If so, lay it before the Holy One and receive His forgiveness. (Read Psalm 38:18 for a simple prayer of confession.) Record your thoughts here.

6. Read Psalm 66:16-20 and describe this scene so that a child could understand. How can you apply these verses in your life?

7. Spend twenty minutes (or as many as you can) in worship and record your thoughts here or in a journal. (Optional worship verses: Psalm 80:1-17.)

DAY 3: SPIRITUAL SENSES

1. Have you ever thought about spiritual senses before, or is this a new concept for you? Read Psalm 95:6-8 and write it here. What are your feelings about this passage?

2. Worship is the bridge between the temporal and the eternal. It is the gateway into God's presence. Read Psalm 89:15 and Psalm 116:9. What does the Old Testament say about entering into God's presence?

3. In light of what you have learned about spiritual senses, explain Acts 28:26-27. Are you able to understand passages like this more clearly? Explain your answer.

4. Read Hebrews 4:16 and Hebrews 10:21-22 and personalize them here. What privilege do believers have, according to the New Testament?

5. Read Psalm 22:26. Make a list of everything you observe about worship in this verse. How can you apply this in your life?

6. Enter into the presence of the Holy One now by spending twenty minutes (or as many as you can) in worship today and record your thoughts here or in a journal. (Optional worship verses: Psalm 103:1-5.)

DAY 4: WRESTLING WITH GOD

1. Is there anything that has hindered your worship in the past few days? Identify these barriers and write a prayer asking God to show you how to remove them.

2. What questions, if any, have kept you from entering into deep intimacy with the Beloved? List them here. Remember that God already knows your heart and is big enough to handle all of your confusion. He wants you to lay your questions down before His throne.

3. The children of Israel wrestled with God throughout the Old Testament even though He gave them specific regulations about their relationship with Him. What did the Lord require of them in Deuteronomy 10:20-21?

4. Are you clinging to Him or wrestling with Him?

5. David often cried out to God in his pain. Read Psalm 5:11 and 59:16 and describe the promise in the Old Testament for those who take refuge in the Lord.

6. Read Hebrews 6:18 and describe the promise in the New Testament for those who take refuge in the Lord.

7. Spend twenty minutes (or as many as you can) in worship today and record your thoughts here or in a journal. (Optional worship verses: Psalm 84:1-4, 9-12.)

DAY 5: WHERE WAS GOD?

1. Have you ever wondered where God is when bad things happen? What are some of the answers you've heard in the past? Describe how this affects the way you feel about God.

2. Read 1 Kings 22:19 and explain the way God describes Himself. Is this the way you envision the Holy One? Explain your answer.

3. Read Psalm 18:9-15 and ask God to show you how He is fighting for you. Record your thoughts here.

4. The Israelites cried out to God for help when they were enslaved in Egypt, and God responded. Read Exodus 4:31 and write it here. How did God feel about their situation? What was the response of the Israelites when they heard this? Do you believe that God feels this same way about you? What should be your response?

5. When you hear the concept of nestling into God, what comes to your mind? If it is hard for you to think about "cuddling" into Him, ask for a safe picture of how you can relate to Him at this point in your journey. Describe it here.

6. Read Jeremiah 32:40 and ask God to put a desire to worship Him in your heart as He promised the Israelites. Spend twenty minutes (or as many as you can) in worship. Record your thoughts here or in a journal.

CHAPTER 4

THE SECRET PLACE

"No, Honey! Don't wanna see Santa!" my two-year-old twin grandsons shrieked.

I was perplexed. "Buddies, remember how much fun you've had with your toy Santa Claus? Remember how nice he is in the books we've been reading? You don't have to be afraid of Santa!"

Hudson and Jackson had been intrigued with Santa Claus for days, waiting excitedly for a face-to-face encounter at the mall. When we first arrived at the photo station, they were happy to observe him interacting with the other children. It seemed like they could have watched for hours—as long as it was from a distance. I was caught completely off guard when they began screaming as I tried to take them closer.

When Christmas arrived, their daddy, Bill, dressed in a Santa costume to surprise the boys. When they saw him they wailed in terror. Then Bill lifted his beard so they could see who he was. Slowly they began to warm up to him. Later that afternoon, I put on the fluffy white beard and red Santa hat in front of the twins. I whisked Hudson up and we chased Jackson, the three of us laughing hysterically. They were delighted by "Santa" when they knew who was behind the beard.

This is what my spiritual life was like for many years. I was intrigued by God and loved to read the Bible and other books about Him. When I was honest, however, I was afraid to get too close to Him. Like Hudson and Jackson, I enjoyed watching God from a distance. But as I met the Holy One in worship, my fear subsided. Now I am finding great delight in the Secret Place, where I am developing my secret life with God:

> You hide them in the secret place of Your presence
> from the conspiracies of man;
> You keep them secretly in a shelter from the strife
> of tongues.
>
> PSALM 31:20, NASB

In this place of shelter I sit at the feet of God with His living Word opened before me. I talk to my heavenly Father and He talks to me in the language of intimate friendship. This is the holy place of divine healing where we are able to see the Lord in a different light. Amazingly, when I came to know the Father for who He really is, I found that He is safe. Then God and I began to find mutual delight in each other, much as I experienced with Hudson and Jackson on that eventful Christmas afternoon.

My playtime with my grandsons pales in comparison to the relationship that God desires for His children to experience with Him. No words can adequately describe what His love is meant to be. It is amazingly wonderful, burning with passion, and so intense that it should take your breath away. It is designed to bring comfort and healing, motivation and guidance, inner peace and joy overflowing. God's love should be the foundation of our life and focus of our attention.

Psychologists have shown that emotional healing can take place when a wounded soul finds comfort in another's loving care. If this is true, then God's love is able to heal every single heart, no matter how shattered and broken it is. So why do so few people experience true joy and genuine pleasure in their relationship with God? Why is it that Scripture speaks so much about His great love for us but most Christians don't experience it? They may have moments of emotional pleasure, but for the most part they either feel guilty and inadequate or become satisfied with a status quo, emotionless relationship with God.

BARRIERS TO THE SECRET PLACE

God created us with a desire for intimacy. His designed Adam and Eve to be a conduit for His love so that love could then be given and received in a pure and unselfish way. But that plan was tragically marred when sin entered the world. God's nature hasn't changed, but our interpretation of it has been warped because of the sinful responses of human beings. As a result, we try to please God by being religious and doing good things for Him—but all He wants is our hearts (Hosea 6:6).

This God-given need for a loving relationship generates a longing for fulfillment that can only be satisfied in Him. Unfortunately, our minds are sometimes thrown out of rhythm because of pain from disappointment and rejection. When this occurs, our ability to feel that we are loved can become obstructed.

Overcoming the devastation caused by past and present pain isn't a simple task. This transformation can occur only when a person chooses to fully embrace and experience the loving comfort of God. It doesn't matter how other people have cared for you or how many times you've been hurt. The love of God is passionate, constant, and unconditional. Even though others may have let you down unintentionally or hurt you maliciously, His love has never ceased or failed. So instead of listening to imperfect human messages of rejection, we need to go to the promises of God in His divine Word to understand the truth.

Intimate means "marked by very close association, contact, or familiarity; marked by a warm friendship developing through long association."[1] We all crave this kind of connection, and although it takes work, it is possible to obtain. The moment each of us accepts Christ as our Savior and enters into a personal relationship with Him, we have intimacy with God, but it is inconsistent. We all face many interruptions and barriers that keep us from enjoying the deep closeness we long for.

THE BARRIER OF RELIGION

Many people believe they need to be religious and do something for God. As humans, we feel better working for God because we think we need to earn His favor. The problem is that there are always more things that need to be done, and we feel disappointed when they aren't done well enough, even if it is only perceived imperfection. I know this from experience—most of my life I strived to keep everyone happy, but there were some people, like my parents, whom I could never please.

It was only natural for me to carry this style of relating into my relationship with my heavenly Father, so I began with good works, but I was always afraid that I would mess up. I ended up majoring on what I could do for God, which always seemed to fall short, so it was impossible to go deeper in my relationship with Him.

Now, there is nothing wrong with obedience and serving. Both are biblical, and God is pleased when we obey His Word: "Through Him then, let us continually offer up a sacrifice of praise to God, that is, the fruit of lips that give thanks to His name. And do not neglect doing good and sharing, for with such sacrifices God is pleased" (Hebrews 13:15-16, NASB).

These verses mention two types of equally important sacrifices. The first is a "sacrifice of praise," and the second is "doing good and sharing." This passage reveals that God "is pleased" when a person begins with a passionate relationship with Him, rather than passionless religious activity. So I begin my day with a "sacrifice of praise" by bowing my heart and using my words to praise Him. Then I get up in an attitude of worship and trust God to lead me throughout the day as I bow my life in service. As A. W. Tozer said, "We're here to be worshippers first and workers only second. . . . The work done by a worshipper will have eternity in it."[2]

The confusion occurs when we put a higher priority on what we can do for God (religious activity) than on what He has done for us (an intimate relationship). When this happens, that which can be a "good thing" becomes skewed. When we obey with our actions rather than with our hearts, our spirituality is merely external. Jesus reprimanded the Pharisees in the New Testament about this: "What sorrow awaits you Pharisees! For you are careful to tithe even the tiniest income from your herb gardens, but you ignore justice and the love of God. You should tithe, yes, but do not neglect the more important things" (Luke 11:42).

These Jewish leaders substituted religion for a relationship with God. This caused them to tragically miss the Messiah, God's greatest gift of love. In order for us to keep from stumbling over this barrier, we must constantly ask ourselves, *Whose glory are we seeking in life—God's or our own?* Jesus told us, "He who speaks from himself seeks his own glory; but He who is seeking the glory of the One who sent Him, He is true, and there is no unrighteousness in Him" (John 7:18, NASB).

The Lord desires for us to serve Him out of a loving relationship rather than duty. Pleasing Him through obedience to His Word will flow out of us when we are assured of His love. When this happens we experience great joy in serving Him and He receives all the glory. The barrier of religion is removed when we know, without a doubt, that we can't do anything that will make God love us any more or any less than He already does.

THE BARRIER OF FEAR

I recently asked several women what was keeping them from going deeper in their relationship with the Lord. Many of them agreed with one woman's brave answer: "I'm closest to God when I'm going through a trial, so I'm afraid that He will cause something bad to happen if I seek an intimate relationship with Him."

Emotional, physical, or spiritual trauma can cause a person to shut down. As a result, some people find it hard, if not impossible, to trust God. Others view Him as a harsh judge who wants to punish them severely. Both of these assumptions stem from a misunderstanding of the true character of God and result in self-protective measures. Until we learn to trust that God's heart is for our good, we will stumble upon this barrier of fear.

I struggled with anxiously trying to please God until I was exhausted. I finally gave in and prayed this simple prayer: *Dear God, I give up!* This was the moment the Holy One had been waiting for. Suddenly the barriers to the Secret Place were removed as I was ushered into the presence of the Holy One.

Since that time, in one sense, I haven't learned a plethora of new facts about God, although it seems as if I've come to truly know Him for the first time in my life. My knowledge of my heavenly Father hasn't been tremendously altered, but my understanding has been dramatically transformed. What I had always known in my mind began to transcend to my heart and now I am able to truly know what I already knew about God.

FACTS OR FEELINGS?

Scripture clearly reveals that God wants us to feel His love. But this doesn't mean that our emotions are what we use as a guide to establish what is true or false about God. Rather, the way we feel about God must stem from the truth found in Scripture.

In Psalm 119, we read: "I run in the path of your command-ments, for you have set my heart free" (verse 32, WEB). The psalm-ist recognized that the passionate pursuit of God's Word and an overflowing love for God go hand in hand. Without this impor-tant union, our good deeds would be simply that: good deeds done with the wrong motive. This is why Jesus was appalled by the scribes and Pharisees who looked good on the outside but were dead on the inside.

Puritan pastor Jonathan Edwards understood the importance of emotions in the spiritual life. He stated, "True religion, in great part, consists in holy affections."[3] He recognized that God has endowed each person with two different relational capabilities: the mind and the heart. The mind is used to perceive, speculate, and discern one's view of things with the intellect. The heart, on the other hand, is the sense by which a person beholds things with the emotions. This is where "holy affections" originate, causing us to be greatly drawn toward someone or to disapprove or reject them. Scripture reveals that God longs for His children to love Him in a passionate way: "You must love the LORD your God with all your heart, all your soul, and all your strength" (Deuteronomy 6:5). "Holy affections" are an outpouring of one's heart toward the Lord. Consequently, the more we know God, the more we love Him. The more we love Him, the more our lives are transformed.

When we spend daily time in worship, something mysterious happens: Our hearts open up to the Lord in an astounding way. Although trials won't magically disappear, the way we view them changes. Inexpressible joy will well up within us as we become captivated by the Lord (1 Peter 1:8).

How do we move from knowing about God and loving Him the best we can, to knowing Him intimately? Experiencing the nearness of God in worship leads us to the Secret Place where our souls, no matter how wounded, can be comforted, sheltered, and restored.

EXPERIENCING MUTUAL DELIGHT

While it is easy for me to understand the many verses in Scripture where we are exhorted to rejoice in the Lord, I am overwhelmed by His passion for me. Zephaniah 3:17 says that God exults over His children with great pleasure and pure delight: "The LORD your God is in your midst, a victorious warrior. He will exult over you with joy, He will be quiet in His love, He will rejoice over you with shouts of joy" (NASB).

The Hebrew word for *exult* means "to be glad, rejoice greatly, joy, make mirth, rejoice."[4] It carries the sense of extreme gladness and festive pleasure. The word *rejoice* comes from a primitive root that means "to spin round under the influence of any violent emotion."[5] This means that God's heart dances around in circles in joyous celebration when He thinks about you. This divine jubilation then shifts to a peaceful, quiet love that is so deeply felt by Him that words are inadequate. Can you believe it? It's as if God is sometimes speechless when He considers His love for His children. It's like He is saying, "I love you so much that I can't find words to express it."

God desires for us to experience mutual delight with Him. Think about what this might look like. Your heavenly Father sings over you, and you sing back to Him. You dance together and experience great pleasure in His warm embrace. Then you go back and forth rejoicing in each other all over again.

Sarah Edwards, wife of Jonathan Edwards, experienced this kind of intimacy with God when revival broke out in the late 1730s and 1740s. After an incredible encounter with the Holy One, she recorded her experiences:

> The great part of the night I lay awake, sometimes asleep,
> and sometimes between sleeping and waking. But all night
> I continued in a constant, clear, and lively sense of the
> heavenly sweetness of Christ's excellent and transcendent

love, of his nearness to me, and of my dearness to him; with an inexpressibly sweet calmness of soul in an entire rest in him. I seemed to myself to perceive a glow of divine love come down from the heart of Christ in heaven, into my heart, in a constant stream, like a stream or pencil of sweet light. At the same time, my heart and soul all flowed out in love to Christ; so that there seemed to be a constant flowing and reflowing of heavenly and divine love, from Christ's heart to mine; and I appeared to myself to float or swim, in these bright, sweet beams of the love of Christ.[6]

God's love is not to be viewed from afar, but to be experienced deeply in an up-close intimate relationship. He desires for all of His children to move from merely knowing that He loves them to experiencing it firsthand. He wants you to feel the joy of being loved—to receive it personally and powerfully in a way that will change your life forever.

A FATHER UNLIKE ANY OTHER

Part of understanding this intimacy with God means understanding who He is as our Father. As you know, I had a huge father wound—and maybe you do too. Our relationship with our earthly father greatly impacts the way we relate to our heavenly Father. Even though I had studied the Scriptures revealing how drastically different Father God is, the only father I knew was my dad, and I transferred my fear of my earthly father to my heavenly Father. This false association resulted in confusion and distrust. I was constantly doing something in an effort to keep Him happy.

This behavior changed as I realized that God is not only my creator but my loving Father. John taught this to the early church: "To all who believed him and accepted him, he gave the right to become children of God" (John 1:12). It is one thing to call God "Father" at the beginning of a prayer; it is quite another thing to experience the comfort, love, and protection of our heavenly Father. No earthly father's love can compare with the love of God (Ephesians 3:18).

You may have had a father who hurt you accidentally or in horrific ways, but our heavenly Father is incapable of evil behavior because He is a father unlike any other. Throughout the Bible, God's character is pure and holy without any blemish (1 Peter 1:15-16). We can trust God implicitly because He is the only one whose heart is always good.

FINDING HEALING IN THE SECRET PLACE

Adoption is the term that Paul used to describe our relationship with God in his letter to the believers in Rome: "You have not received a spirit of slavery leading to fear again, but you have received a spirit of adoption as sons by which we cry out, 'Abba! Father!'" (Romans 8:15, NASB). When Paul wrote these words, adoption referred to the legal action in which an adult took a child who was not his own into his family, with the purpose of treating him as his own child. This child was legally entitled to all the rights and privileges of a natural-born child. Similarly, when we trust in Christ, we are adopted and placed in a new family. This divine privilege includes a new name, as well as everything that belongs to Christ (Colossians 1:27).

When our heavenly Father adopted us, He assumed the legal role of caregiver. Therefore, He will be with us always, in the good and the bad (2 Corinthians 4:8-9). Though we are pressed into a tight space where there is no way out, our heavenly Father will hold us in His strong arms so that we won't be crushed. We may become confused and temporarily forget the way, but if we keep seeking God, He will be our refuge. We may be treated harshly, but He will always be on our side. And when we get knocked down, He is there to pick us up and get us back on our feet again. He will never abandon us.

My oldest niece, Melody, suffered the shattering blow of tragedy. The love of the Father kept her from falling into a generational pattern of mental illness:

Change and upheaval were the norm in my life as a child. My dad was a raging alcoholic for as long as I can remember. He married four times, with my mom being his first and last wife. Our home was characterized by violence and infidelity that caused me to constantly search for a place to hide. I remember shaking in fear under the coffee table, terrified that my mom was going to die. It is an image in my mind that still haunts me.

People that I loved came in and out of my life due to my dad's anger and disassociation with them. We went for years without speaking to my dad's relatives, who were one of my only safe refuges. This horrific loss was heart-wrenching for me and caused me to have stomach problems. After years of being married to other people, my mom and dad remarried. In time, however, my dad's anger and mental illness led to the tragedy I had always feared. In a moment of inexplicable passion, my dad killed my mother and committed suicide. To add to our suffering, my brother committed suicide with the same gun a few years later.

The catastrophic loss of my parents and brother could have destroyed me, but God had other plans. I could have become bitter or despondent, but He saved me from my past and from a future filled with sadness and defeat. I invited Christ into my heart at a young age, and as I worked through my pain, God revealed Himself as my heavenly Father whom I could trust. Although I was devastated by my losses, I was able to understand how much God loves me and that He has been with me always. Even though my earthly dad caused turmoil and destruction in my life, my heavenly Father has brought redemption to my painful circumstances.

Melody found comfort knowing that she was adopted by her heavenly Father. It wasn't easy, but she pressed into Him and found His heart in the midst of her pain.

When I finally understood what it meant to be adopted by my heavenly Father, something miraculous happened. For the first time in my life I believed these words in the book of James:

> Whatever is good and perfect is a gift coming down to us from God our Father, who created all the lights in the heavens. He never changes or casts a shifting shadow. He chose to give birth to us by giving us his true word. And we, out of all creation, became his prized possession.
>
> JAMES 1:17-18

Charla Pereau is an American missionary who runs an orphanage in Mexico. Several years ago, she and her husband adopted a Zapotec Indian baby named Charles Curtis. After an eye exam, they were surprised to find that he had astigmatism. Charla's husband said, "How can this be? Nobody in the Pereau family or your family has ever had to wear glasses."[7] Even though their son looked very different from the rest of the family, his father no longer saw him as the little Indian boy they had adopted. He had become one of their prized family members.

This is the way our heavenly Father views us when we are adopted into His family. He has completely forgotten where we came from and what we have done in our past. We have become permanent members of His family, and He sees us with a father's loving eyes.

Perhaps your father was a wonderful, safe person, but no earthly father is without flaw. The Secret Place is where all of our father wounds can be healed and restored. In chapter 1 we saw that everyone longs to return to joy. The Bible clearly reveals the most amazing revelation that will finally bring comfort to your father wound. You, precious child, are the sparkle in your heavenly Father's eye. He has adopted you and will never abandon or reject you. He is waiting with eager anticipation to embrace you and give you comfort so that you can return to joy. He is inviting you to come and find healing in the Secret Place.

> Even if my father and mother abandon me,
>   the LORD will hold me close.
>
> PSALM 27:10

THE SECRET PLACE
STUDY

DAY 1: THE SECRET PLACE

1. How did you feel about God the Father before reading this chapter?

2. Read Psalm 27:5 and Psalm 31:20. What do these verses say that God will do when we face trouble? Where do you think this is and how do you get there?

3. Where does the Father abide according to Matthew 6:6? Where do you think this is?

4. Do you feel like the Secret Place of God is safe? Why or why not?

5. Have you enjoyed reading the Bible and other books about God but have been unable to feel close to Him? Explain your answer.

6. Listen to worship songs about God's love this week. Play them over and over, allowing His healing love to wash over you. Record your thoughts here or in a journal.

DAY 2: BARRIERS TO THE SECRET PLACE

1. Has religion been a barrier for you in the past or present? If so, what do you need to do to move forward?

2. What does Psalm 103:13-14 say about God? Describe how this knowledge affects your heart.

3. Read Psalm 28:6-7 and personalize it, using your own name and expanding on it in your own words.

4. Do you believe this is true for you? If not, ask the Holy One to help you receive it as truth.

5. Has fear been a barrier for you in the past or present? If so, what do you need to do to move forward?

6. Read 1 John 5:18-20 and personalize these verses here. Use the words *I* and *me* to state what is true of God and you. Ask the Holy One to help you truly know what you already know about this.

7. Intimacy with the Father cannot be attained by trying harder, working longer, or making promises. You must press into the Secret Place of the Father to find healing. Read James 4:8 and Jeremiah 29:13. Worship and ask the Father to help you find His heart. Record your thoughts here or in a journal.

DAY 3: FACTS OR FEELINGS?

1. What does intimacy with the Father look like to you? Is it something you are afraid of, or do you long for a deeper relationship with Him?

2. Read Exodus 34:14 and Jeremiah 29:11. What do these verses say about God's heart? Does this surprise you? Explain how this knowledge affects your life.

3. The healing journey is arduous work and frightening at times. What does Deuteronomy 1:29-31 reveal about the way God led the children of Israel? What encouragement do you find in these verses?

4. Read Psalm 40:6-8 and Matthew 22:37. How do these verses go together? What does this mean to you personally?

5. What does Deuteronomy 11:22 say we should do to demonstrate our love for God? What does this look like in your life? (Read this verse in the New Living Translation if possible.)

6. Spend twenty minutes (or as many as you can) in worship and record your thoughts here or in a journal. (Optional worship verses: Psalm 63:1-5.)

DAY 4: EXPERIENCING MUTUAL DELIGHT

1. Read Zephaniah 3:17. Personalize this verse using the literal meanings of the Hebrew words for "exult" and "rejoice" listed on page 66.

2. Read God's promises to Israel in Isaiah 46:3-4. As believers, we are grafted into God's family, and He has the same fatherly affections for us. Do you find delight in your heavenly Father and believe that He delights in you? Explain your answer.

3. Describe how your relationship with your earthly father has affected your relationship with your heavenly Father in both positive and negative ways.

4. When do you feel the most loved by God and why?

5. Read through Psalm 37:23-24 and personalize these verses here. How does this knowledge change the way you see your heavenly Father?

6. What does 1 John 3:1 say about being adopted by our heavenly Father? How does it describe His love for you? Describe how this makes you feel.

7. Your heavenly Father will never reject or abandon you. Read 2 Corinthians 4:8-9 and personalize it. Do you believe this is true for you? How does this change the way you view trials?

8. Read Psalm 25:4-5 and spend time in worship asking the Holy One to show you the path to the Secret Place. Record your thoughts here or in a journal.

DAY 5: FINDING HEALING IN THE SECRET PLACE

1. Ephesians 3:17-19 describes the overflowing love the Father
   has for you. Read these verses and use them to describe
   what it means to be "the sparkle in your Father's eye."

2. Express in a creative way the promises found in Psalm
   25:14 and John 14:21. You can draw or paint a picture;
   choreograph a dance; make a collage; or write a poem,
   song, children's book, or letter expressing the joy of these
   promises. (Use your imagination.)

3. How has this chapter changed the way you view God the
   Father?

4. Spend time worshiping God, our heavenly Father. Record
   your thoughts here or in a journal. (Optional worship
   verses: Psalm 147:1-11.)

CHAPTER 5

THE BRIDGE TO ROMANCE

AHHH . . . romance. I love romance, but what I think is romantic may be different from the norm. Romance is the beautiful hour when the sun is setting and the glory of God bursts forth in the rainbow-lit sky. It is the card or e-mail reminding me that I am special to someone. It can even be surprising little interludes in my day-to-day routine as I catch divine kisses softly blown down from heaven.

Since I love romance, weddings are one of my favorite things in life. Along with the day when I became a Christian and when my children and grandchildren were born, my wedding day was one of the highlights of my life. I felt like my love for my husband, Gary, was unlike any other. I couldn't wait to become his wife. Even though my father tried to sabotage this special occasion with one of his fits of anger, I was so thrilled to become Mrs. Gary DeSalvo that nothing could spoil this special day. Amazingly, I was able to laugh it off when Dad threatened my new husband soon after we were pronounced man and wife. Instead of being embarrassed and devastated, I was able to rejoice because I had a husband to love and protect me.

It doesn't matter if it is a simple or extremely elaborate affair;

the joy of seeing two people in love makes me sigh in delight. One of Jesus' most amazing promises is that we can experience divine romance in our everyday life. Heaven will be beyond description, but we don't have to wait until we die to experience His captivating presence. Authors Dee Brestin and Kathy Troccoli speak about this: "As a member of the relational sex, we long to be loved, we long to be cherished. And we are very interested in romance, in stories where the hero deeply loves and sacrifices for the lady. God knows this, for He made us. And He knows how to talk to us. The whole Bible can be viewed as a wonderful romance."[1]

Come with me to learn about the ultimate wedding as we cross the Bridge to Romance.

THE ULTIMATE WEDDING

The image of a glorious wedding is seen throughout the New Testament, describing the relationship of Jesus to the church. It is a perfect picture, from beginning to end, of the romance between Christ and His bride. The apostle Paul said, "I am jealous for you with the jealousy of God himself. I promised you as a pure bride to one husband—Christ" (2 Corinthians 11:2). Jesus, our Bridegroom, is making preparations for a great wedding celebration. Believers fulfill the role of the bride in this divine matrimony. Jesus initiates and we respond. He gives generously and we receive. He gently leads us and we follow with joy (some of the time). He loves us first and we reciprocate by giving our hearts to Him with intoxicating desire and joyful delight.

This is a royal wedding, far more glorious than the most extravagant noble marriage in all of history. In the Scriptures Jesus is given the title "King of kings," which indicates His royal position. Believe it or not, this regal King has chosen you to be His beloved. Even though there is no royal lineage in my family, He chose me as His bride. This thrills my soul and causes my love for Him to burst forth with emotion.

Jesus has pledged His love to believers in a passionate way. Examining the ancient Jewish marriage customs helps us understand the truth of our Savior's intentional, deep love for His bride.

CHOOSING THE BRIDE

The engagement period in the ancient Near East culture involved specific steps. Usually the families of the couple arranged the marriage, but the man could also make his personal preference known to his parents. However, his father had the ultimate say in the matter. In the holy union between Jesus and the church, God is the heavenly Father of both Christ, the groom, and the church, His bride, .

There are two types of churches. One is a visible church, which is the assembly of Christians gathered for worship in a religious meeting. These are the individual church bodies that meet around the world, including the ones that you and I belong to. The other is the true church, which refers to everyone who has accepted Christ as their Savior. The true church represents all believers around the world, past, present, and future. You and I are individual members of this true church if we have entered into a relationship with Christ (Ephesians 1:23).

While none can deny that Jesus is the perfect bridegroom, completely acceptable by the Father, the thought of God approving me as a bride for Jesus is unfathomable. Throughout Scripture, God uses humbling terms to describe humankind: lost, dead, foolish, unfaithful. But He also calls us His sons (and daughters), beloved, chosen ones. One of the most endearing of all the terms used to describe the church is "the bride, the wife of the Lamb" (Revelation 21:9).

Just think what this means! Every single person, both male and female, is the beloved bride of Jesus if they have accepted Him as their personal Savior.

THE MARRIAGE COVENANT

Although Western culture doesn't understand the Hebraic significance of covenants, this matter is very important to God. Throughout biblical history, when God decided to restore a relationship with humankind He did it through a covenant, which is much more than a contract or legal document. The marriage covenant was one of many. This ceremony took place over a meal between the two families of the bride and groom and included four significant cups of wine. The first was shared by the two families, symbolizing their commitment to serve as one family. The second was shared between the bride and groom and their fathers, usually after long and heated discussions over the marriage contract. During this time, a bride price was agreed upon. In ancient times the groom's family was expected to pay a bride price to the bride's parents. This payment was required by law as compensation for the cost of raising her. The amount reflected the perceived value of the bride and could be tendered either with cash or by working the payment out.

What was the bride price required in the marriage covenant between Christ and the church? It was the greatest bride token ever paid in history, although it couldn't be measured in gold or silver. The costly fee was the sacrifice of Jesus' life, given to pay for the sins of His betrothed. We see this in 1 Peter: "For you know that it was not with perishable things such as silver or gold that you were redeemed from the empty way of life handed down to you from your ancestors, but with the precious blood of Christ, a lamb without blemish or defect" (1 Peter 1:18-19, NIV).

Do you feel as though you are unworthy? You aren't alone. The evil one desires for all of us to feel like Christ would never want us for His bride, but I have some important news for you. Every single one of us has some kind of baggage that can make us feel hopelessly inadequate, pitifully worthless, and totally unacceptable. All of us have sinned. We were born in a state of rebellion against God and have missed the mark in some way. It doesn't matter if you have hurt someone, had an abortion, or simply told a little white lie. In God's eye, sin is sin (Romans 3:23). None of us is more or less worthy than another. But Christ's sacrifice makes us worthy.

In the ancient marriage covenant, after everything about the bride price was agreed upon, the bridegroom poured the third cup of wine for his beloved to offer the marriage covenant. If the woman agreed to the proposal, she would accept the cup and drink the wine, making their engagement official.

When I understood that I was separated from God because of my sin, I could hardly wait to be reconciled. So when Jesus offered the cup of salvation to me, I accepted it with inexpressible gratitude. I stepped across the vast chasm separating me from the Father, which was my sin, and found that Jesus truly is the Bridge to Romance.

THE FATHER'S WEDDING GIFT

As far back as the time of Christ, it was customary for a good father to give a portion of the bride price to his daughter as a bridal gift. In addition, if the father could afford it, he gave his daughter parting gifts to help equip the bride for her new life. Scripture speaks of parcels of land and female slaves given as dowries to take into a bride's new home (Genesis 24:59).

Similarly, when I entered the marriage covenant with Christ, my heavenly Father gave me a gift worth far more than any earthly thing. He forgave my sin and gave me a clean heart. We see this in the book of Romans: "There is a great difference between Adam's sin and God's gracious gift. For the sin of this one man, Adam, brought death to many. But even greater is God's wonderful grace and his gift of forgiveness to many through this other man, Jesus Christ" (5:15).

This means that Jesus, as our Bridegroom, paid the immeasurable bride price for us, and our heavenly Father gave us the extravagant gift of forgiveness. It doesn't matter to Him what has happened in the past, good or bad. He now sees us through eyes of love. Like a fairy tale come true, He wanted us and we wanted Him, so we joined our hearts together in a romantic betrothal. This is a pure and holy romance—the greatest love story ever told.

Ruthie struggled to find herself in the midst of this love story:

"God hates divorce" (Malachi 2:16) echoed in my ears. I was in my late forties when I accepted Christ, so I had much to learn. My studies taught me that the Lord had forgiven my sins, but because I was in my second marriage I felt like I was a second-class Christian.

I would cringe when asked, "How long have you been married?" Even worse was when someone asked, "How many children do you have?" Although I had desperately wanted to have a baby, I was never able to conceive. Not only were my arms empty and my heart broken, I read in the Old Testament that barrenness was a sign to others that sin and disobedience were present in my life. The father of lies used this to make me believe that the Lord had withheld the privilege of motherhood from me as a way of showing His displeasure.

As I continued in my quest to understand God's Word, I saw that God's character is full of mercy and grace and that Jesus has paid the price in full for my sins. With this knowledge I was able to lay my guilt and shame at the foot of the cross. I now see my worth reflected in the Savior's love for me instead of what the world thinks. As a result, my past no longer defines me. I now cling to His Truth: I am a "new creation . . . the old has gone, the new is here!" (2 Corinthians 5:7, NIV).

Like Ruthie, as our understanding of the Savior begins to shift from our minds to our hearts, we come to truly know what we already knew about Jesus. When we finally comprehend the fervent heart of our Bridegroom, we are able to experience a captivating relationship with the lover of our souls.

RESPONSIBILITIES OF THE GROOM

The prospective bride and groom in ancient times were legally bound together after the betrothal covenant was agreed upon. During this period the terms *husband* and *wife* were used, although the couple didn't live together. The groom then departed to prepare their new home, but not before assuring his bride that that he would return to consummate the marriage and complete the marriage ceremony. It usually took him about a year to build an addition onto his father's house as a labor of love for his bride.

Knowing that He was leaving soon, Jesus comforted His disciples by saying,

> Don't let your hearts be troubled. Trust in God, and
> trust also in me. There is more than enough room in
> my Father's home. If this were not so, would I have told
> you that I am going to prepare a place for you? When
> everything is ready, I will come and get you, so that you
> will always be with me where I am.   JOHN 14:1-3

Even though the disciples were in emotional turmoil over the thought of Jesus leaving, they understood what this meant. It was the promise that a bridegroom would make to his betrothed. While it seemed like their world was falling apart, they were urged to do the very thing that seemed impossible: to believe that He would return for them. He was not rejecting or abandoning them, as it might appear. On the contrary, He was taking pre-eminent care of them by preparing a place where they could abide with Him forever. As Randy Alcorn describes,

The return of Christ will signal not only the Father rescuing his children but also the Bridegroom rescuing his bride. As the church, we're part of the ultimate Cinderella story—rescued from a home where we labor, often without appreciation or reward. One day we'll be taken into the arms of the Prince and whisked away to live in his palace.[2]

When we are going through trials in life, we are encouraged to remember that we have a Beloved Bridegroom preparing a bridal chamber for us in heaven. There is immense security in knowing that the lover of our souls will never abandon us, no matter what. When our eyes are locked on our Bridegroom, we are able to experience divine comfort that helps us return to joy.

RESPONSIBILITIES OF THE BRIDE

During ancient times, the bride also had responsibilities to prepare for her wedding ceremony. This included taking purifying baths, so that she would be found clean and untainted by her bridegroom upon his return (as we see in the book of Esther), and wearing the proper bridal attire.

As the bride of Christ, we must be cleansed for Jesus. Unfortunately, this kind of purification cannot be accomplished by any type of spa package, no matter how fabulous it is. Only a spiritual bath can cleanse our hearts and make us acceptable from the inside out. The apostle Paul explained this:

> For husbands, this means love your wives, just as Christ loved the church. He gave up his life for her to make her holy and clean, washed by the cleansing of God's word. He did this to present her to himself as a glorious church without a spot or wrinkle or any other blemish. Instead, she will be holy and without fault. EPHESIANS 5:25-27

Christ is the one who cleans our hearts, so what is our responsibility in this cleansing process? We must turn away from our sinful actions and move toward God and His truth (Acts 3:19). We do this by confessing our sin to Him and receiving His forgiveness. Then we turn away from the things that go against the nature of God and live in a way that is pleasing to Him. When we mess up, we ask for forgiveness and choose to do the right thing instead. This results in divine cleansing from the Holy One.

Bob Sorge offers great insight about repentance:

> It is in the secret place that I find "my spirit makes
> diligent search" (Psalm 77:6). I so very much long to
> please Him and to know His will, so my spirit diligently
> searches the recesses of my heart to see if there might
> be anything in me for which I need to repent. I want
> nothing of my self-life to hinder my relationship with
> Him or His purposes for us together.[3]

The next responsibility of the ancient Jewish bride was wearing the proper bridal attire as an outward sign that she was officially betrothed, even though her groom was away. This meant wearing a bridal veil made with loving stitches that far outweighed any monetary value.

Modern brides may spend thousands of dollars to purchase the perfect bridal attire, even though it's usually worn for a single day and then stored in a closet, if not sold or given away. But the wedding garment that God desires for us cannot be purchased with any amount of money. Miraculously, it is a free gift from our Beloved and will last for all eternity.

The Holy One has clothed His bride in a divine garment that is costly beyond measure. He has placed upon her head a sparkling crown of forgiveness shining brightly with His glory.

His love covers us with His righteousness (Colossians 3:14), and we are now seen in light of what He has done to secure us as His chosen bride.

The Scarlet Letter tells the story of a woman named Hester Prynne who lived in the Puritan settlement of Boston in the seventeenth century. After being found guilty of committing adultery, she was sentenced to wear the scarlet letter *A* on her chest. She was forced to wear a garment that would never let her forget that she was an adulteress.

Like Hester's *A*, shame is the clothing of many men and women today. We try our best to hide it, but it is always lurking in the darkness, reminding us of our greatest fear: that we are worthless and undesired. In time, Satan's lies seem so real that we believe they are who we are, and we put on an invisible garment of shame that will never let us forget the past. Even though it seems absurd, we sometimes feel more comfortable wearing these nasty old rags because we have become so accustomed to them. The Holy One desires for us to cast off every garment of shame, once and for all, and revel in the dazzling new bridal clothes that He has graciously provided.

God gave the prophet Isaiah these words to Israel, but they can also bring healing to each of His children:

Fear not; you will no longer live in shame.
　　　Don't be afraid; there is no more disgrace for you.
You will no longer remember the shame of your
　　　　　youth
　　　　and the sorrows of widowhood.
For your Creator will be your husband;
　　　the LORD of Heaven's Armies is his name!
He is your Redeemer, the Holy One of Israel,
　　　the God of all the earth.

ISAIAH 54:4-5

Are you ready to be bathed in the holiness of the Lord, or do you feel like your sin is so despicable that it's beyond exoneration? Perhaps you believe that God has forgiven you, but you can't forgive yourself. It doesn't matter what you've done or what's been done to you, no matter how horrific it may have been. God desires for you to be unashamed before Him with no stain of sin (Ephesians 5:25-27), clothed in pure white bridal clothes.

THE CONSUMMATION OF THE MARRIAGE

In ancient biblical times, after the bridal chamber was completed, the bridegroom would come for his bride and consummate their marriage. This was a holy union where these two separate beings became so physically bonded and emotionally and spiritually connected that in God's eyes they became one flesh.

Amazingly, the sexual union between a husband and wife is a picture of the spiritual oneness between Christ and the church. It is a glimpse of the divine love relationship that God desires to have with His children (Ephesians 5:31-32). We become one with Christ when we enter into a divine marriage, and we should live our lives in the afterglow of the most divine intimacy possible.

THE BRIDAL CELEBRATION

After the marriage was consummated, there was a joyous celebration filled with eating, drinking, dancing, and rejoicing to conclude the ancient wedding ceremony. The fourth and final cup of wine was shared at this time, symbolizing the eternal union of the marriage covenant. This event would be remembered for a lifetime.

Likewise, our hearts should be filled with overflowing jubilation as we celebrate our union with our Beloved. Unfortunately, it is not possible to manufacture passionate love for Him. When we try to force our emotions to well up for Christ, we end up focusing on what we can do for Him instead of simply focusing on Him.

As in any intimate relationship, we must make Christ a priority, which means spending time and energy to make love blossom.

Before Jesus ascended into heaven He promised His disciples, "Be sure of this: I am with you always, even to the end of the age" (Matthew 28:20). Once again those two simple words, *with you*, contain healing power. Though others may fail you, Jesus is the ultimate Bridegroom who loves you with a passionate, holy love. This means that we don't have to wait until Jesus returns to fully enjoy Him—we can have the joy and comfort of experiencing Him here with us on earth.

Kay found comfort in the heart of her Beloved when her husband died unexpectedly. She celebrates her Bridegroom like few women I've ever known:

> As the stark reality of Charles's death sank deeper into my soul, I began to realize the unspeakable depth of my loss: friend, lover, confidant, spiritual leader. Yet deeper sadness pervaded the day I recognized another dimension of his absence: Now there is no one to pray for me the way he did. I no sooner finished this thought than the Lord whispered to my spirit, "Kay, I am always praying for you." In that moment I knew that He would be a husband to me in every area of my life.
>
> Whether in complicated family matters or in the daily hassles of life, He is a loving, faithful heavenly husband in joys and sorrows. One day I was pushing a grocery cart to the car with a heavy bag of dog food and I said, "Now, Lord, if Charles was here he would put this in the car for me." As I lifted the trunk, a gentleman asked, "May I get that for you?" I'm sure he wondered why my eyes filled with tears as I thanked him.
>
> My Bridegroom is always caring for me, and I celebrate because I've found intimacy like I've never known before.

Are you able to celebrate your Bridegroom like Kay? When we experience His divine comfort and care, we can return to joy.

BRIDEZILLA

Bridezillas is a reality television series that chronicles the lives of women who are engaged to be married . . . and are dominating, bullying, and emotional.

Sometimes our passionate Bridegroom ends up with a disenchanted bride. We transform into Bridezilla when we place the concerns of others over the Lord and fail to give Him the honor He's due. This morphing process can be so discreet that we don't realize it is happening. Like every bridegroom, He longs for His betrothed to love Him in a way that shows He is the most important person in her life. The Old Testament says that He jealously desires to be the first priority in our lives: "You must worship no other gods, for the LORD, whose very name is Jealous, is a God who is jealous about his relationship with you" (Exodus 34:14).

The word *jealous* is defined as "careful in guarding or keeping" and is a derivative of *zealous*, which means "ardent devotion." The Lord's jealousy stems from a heart that is ardently devoted to His beloved.

Are you making the Lord jealous by placing anything before Him? Other relationships, activities, even good things like ministry can become a problem if they take first priority in your life.

SATISFYING SOUL HUNGER

Whether we hunger for love, significance, or pleasure, we all hunger for something. This longing is sometimes referred to as "soul hunger." Far too often, when people feel isolated and lonely, they look to someone else to fill their emptiness. But Jesus is the nourishment that brings lasting fulfillment in life: "Jesus replied, 'I am the bread of life. Whoever comes to me will never be hungry again. Whoever believes in me will never be thirsty'" (John 6:35).

Until our desire for true romance with our Beloved Bridegroom exceeds all other passions, we will never experience lasting fulfillment. Our broken hearts cannot be mended until we find comfort in His loving embrace. It is healthy to face the pain in our souls, to feel the hurt from past violations, to feel bad about past wrongs we have committed, and to admit how desperately we long to feel loved and accepted, but we need to remember that the focus of our relationship with God is not on us. It is on the God who cares for us. We exist for Him—not the other way around.

When we respond to our Lover's overtures of unconditional love, we'll find that our names are written upon His heart. We will experience the sheer delight of standing fully accepted in the presence of our Beloved Bridegroom, and we will return to joy.

Perhaps someone in your life has fulfilled your every desire for romance, but no human being is without flaw. As we continue walking the broken road to intimacy, the most important question we should ask is not, "How can I solve my problems?" but rather, "How can I develop a burning passion for my Beloved so that all of my other concerns become secondary?" When you cross the Bridge to Romance, you will find healing in the magnificent love story you have always longed for but never dreamed possible. This is where every wound from a spouse or other intimate relationship can be healed.

> The Spirit and the bride say, "Come." Let anyone who hears this say, "Come." Let anyone who is thirsty come. Let anyone who desires drink freely from the water of life. REVELATION 22:17

THE BRIDGE TO ROMANCE STUDY

DAY 1: THE ULTIMATE WEDDING

1. How do you feel when you hear the word *romance*? Describe both positive and negative thoughts here.

2. God created you for intimacy, and He longs for you to respond to Him in an intimate way. Read Ephesians 1:4-8 and personalize it by putting in "I," "me," and your own name.

3. Does this change the way you view God's heart for you? Explain your answer.

4. How did Jesus respond to Pilate's accusation in John 18:37? What does this say about your Bridegroom? What does this mean to you personally?

5. What does 2 Corinthians 8:9 say about your Bridegroom? What is your response to this truth?

6. Spend some time worshiping your royal Bridegroom and record your thoughts here or in a journal. (Optional worship verses: Psalm 47.)

DAY 2: CHOOSING THE BRIDE

1. Read Ephesians 1:11-14 and personalize it. How does this make you feel?

2. What does Ephesians 3:19 say about Christ's love for you? How does this affect you?

3. Read 1 Thessalonians 1:4. How do you feel about Jesus choosing you as a bride? Explain your answer.

4. Read 2 Thessalonians 3:5 to see that God was pleased for you to be the bride of Christ. Does this help you understand God's love in a deeper way? Write a prayer expressing your feelings with this verse in mind.

5. Use Ephesians 2:1-10 to write a love message from Jesus to you. Do you believe this is true?

6. Spend time worshiping God and praising Him for choosing you to be the bride of Christ, and record your thoughts here or in a journal. (Optional worship verses: Psalm 66:1-9.)

DAY 3: THE MARRIAGE COVENANT

1. Read 1 John 4:10 and personalize it here. According to this verse, what is "real love"? What is your response to this truth?

2. The marriage of Christ and the church is truly the greatest love story of all time. Read John 15:13 and describe the impact this has on your life.

3. In ancient times the bridegroom offered a cup of wine to the woman of his choice to see if she would accept his proposal. Jesus also offers the cup of salvation to us. What does Acts 3:18-20 say that we need to do in order to demonstrate our acceptance?

4. Can you remember a time when you accepted God's offer of salvation through Christ and entered into a personal relationship with Him? This is not when you were baptized, joined a church, or did any other physical thing. It is an internal decision. Describe what happened here. (If you have not entered into a personal relationship with Christ and would like to know how to do this, see page 209).

5. What is the Father's amazing gift when you accept the cup of salvation according to 1 John 1:9?

6. Meditate on the Father's amazing gift of forgiveness and worship Him. Record your thoughts here or in a journal. (Optional worship verses: Psalm 34:1-10.)

DAY 4: MARITAL RESPONSIBILITIES

Responsibilities of the Groom

1. Do you have a better understanding about what Jesus
   meant in John 14:1-3 after reading about the groom's
   responsibilities in this chapter? Explain your answer.

2. Jesus told the disciples that He was going to prepare a
   place for them and promised that He would return. Read
   Romans 8:38-39 and describe how these verses confirm
   this promise.

Responsibilities of the Bride

1. One of the bride's responsibilities was to take cleansing
   baths. How are we cleansed and made holy according
   to Colossians 1:19-22? How do you feel about this truth?

2. The ancient bride also prepared and wore bridal attire
   as she waited for her groom to return. According to
   Acts 13:38-39, what do you need to do in order to wear
   sparkling bridal apparel?

3. Do you believe that the Holy One has forgiven your sins?
   Have you been able to forgive yourself? If not, what is
   keeping you from doing so?

4. What does Galatians 3:26-27 say that we should "put on" as God's children? How would you explain this in your own words?

5. If you are still wearing your nasty garments of shame, are you willing to discard them today? How will you do this? Explain your answer.

6. "Those who look to him for help will be radiant with joy; no shadow of shame will darken their faces" (Psalm 34:5). Worship the Holy One and ask God to help you understand fully what this verse means. Record your thoughts here or in a journal.

DAY 5: THE CONSUMMATION OF THE MARRIAGE

1. Jesus prayed for all believers throughout history before He went to be with the Father. What was His desire for them in John 17:20-26? Are you experiencing this kind of unity with the Lord and other believers? If not, what do you need to do?

2. God desires for us to celebrate the wedding feast. Read 1 Peter 1:8 and personalize it. Are you experiencing this kind of inexpressible joy? Explain your answer.

3. Read Psalm 68:6. Why do we need to celebrate according to this verse?

4. In light of this lesson, whose family has God placed you in? How does this truth change the way you view yourself?

5. After reading about the Jewish wedding celebration in this chapter, what do you think John the Baptist meant in John 3:29?

6. Have you ever been "Bridezilla" in your relationship with Christ? Explain your answer.

7. Have you ever experienced "soul hunger" as described on page 91? What does Jesus say about this hunger in John 6:35? Is He enough for you, or are you still searching for something more?

8. How has this chapter changed the way you view Jesus, the Bridegroom? Worship your Bridegroom and record your thoughts here or in a journal. (Optional worship verses: 1 Chronicles 16:10-11.)

CHAPTER 6

UNDER HIS SHADOW

I DON'T REMEMBER EXACTLY what had happened, only that I was about five years old and felt lonely and afraid. I longed for someone to hold me close and make me feel safe, but even though there were people around me, none of them seemed to care.

My mother would be the natural person to fill that role, but I learned at an early age that she would become irritated when I needed something from her. So I bottled up my feelings and pretended like I was fine. But I wasn't fine. I was desperate for someone to hold me close and comfort me. I wanted to feel cherished, but my parents acted like they didn't want me. And to be honest, in time I stopped caring. It hurt too much to have unfulfilled expectations. It was easier if I didn't want anything from anyone.

Even though I'm all grown up, I still feel "little" and lonely at times. I am loved and cared for by many people, yet a familiar ache can catch me off guard and hover over me like a dark cloud. A faint memory from the past rears its ugly head and casts a gloomy shadow over me, and all of a sudden I am hit by a storm that leaves me feeling lonely and rejected. My joy is stolen in a matter of seconds.

Mary, the mother of Jesus, was waiting expectantly while her fiancé was preparing a home for her. Like many brides, she probably spent hours daydreaming of the life awaiting her. This ordinary Jewish girl had everyday thoughts about her future, but God had other plans. Her world was turned upside down when God's messenger announced that she was going to give birth to the Messiah. Instead of a dark rain cloud hovering over her, however, Luke tells us that she was overshadowed by the Holy Spirit (Luke 1:35). The word *overshadow* in this verse means "to envelop in a shadow." The psalmist also found comfort from being "under the shadow" of the Holy Spirit (Psalm 91:1-4, AMPC).

These verses promise that we can find safety and comfort in the shadow of the Holy One. I love what Jill Briscoe says about this: "Then the wonderful shadow seemed to wrap itself around me and hold me close into God, as if it were a warm, comforting heavenly blanket."[1] What a powerful picture of comfort! He is the One in whom my soul can safely rest. There is no place for loneliness, sadness, or any other dark cloud when I am resting safely Under His Shadow.

We have seen that God is our heavenly Father who will never reject or abandon us, so we can find healing from every type of father wound as we delight in Him. We have also seen that Jesus is our Bridegroom and that every relational wound can be healed as we bask in His indescribable love for us. But who is this baffling Holy Spirit who overshadows us with divine comfort? What does it mean to rest Under His Shadow?

I've been puzzled by the Holy Spirit for most of my spiritual life. Just the name "Spirit" indicates something mysterious. When I was a little girl the King James Version of the Bible, which was used in most churches, referred to the Holy Spirit as "the Holy Ghost." Now I don't know about you, but I've always been leery of ghosts, so my first impression of this person of the Trinity was confusing. I mistakenly thought He was a vapor or mist without any kind of recognizable form, and I wasn't sure I wanted to meet Him. As a result, I made the grave mistake of neglecting the Holy Spirit for many years.

Thankfully, as I matured, I began to understand that the Holy Spirit is not merely an influence or an impersonal power emanating from God. He is a person, even though I can't see Him with my physical eyes. As the third member of the Trinity, He is equal in every way to God the Father and God the Son. The Bible teaches that the Spirit of God is the divine power by whom we can be liberated and experience the fullness of all that God desires for us. That sounds great, but what does it look like in our everyday experience?

God longs for us to know and trust in all of who He is as the Holy Trinity, but it is easier for me to understand and relate to God the Father and Jesus the Son. Because we can't comprehend the Holy Spirit with our five senses, it's natural for us as human beings to think of Him as an invisible and impersonal entity. In fact, I have heard people mistakenly refer to the Holy Spirit as "It." We must use our spiritual senses, yet again, for enlightenment. Then we will find that He is the Spirit of God: a person in spirit form with an altogether captivating personality. In fact, the Bible reveals that He has emotions, like all of us, and is able to love, be wounded by, rejoice with, speak to, and nurture those whom He loves. Because of this, we can have a very real and intimate relationship with Him. Yet we have to be the one to initiate because He is kind and gentle and will never force Himself on anyone.

If you are having a hard time understanding the mysterious personality of the Holy Spirit, then ask Jesus to help you. There is nothing wrong with being honest with Him. Even Jesus' disciples, who had witnessed the miraculous works of their beloved friend and teacher, struggled at times with their faith. The book of Luke tells us they were overwhelmed by the cost of discipleship and humbly begged Him to help them believe: "The apostles said to the Lord, 'Increase our faith!'" (Luke 17:5, NASB).

Like the apostles, we need to beseech the Holy One to show us how to relate to the Holy Spirit. We must hunger for a deeper understanding of the invisible things of God and continually search the Word with an open mind and heart. Ask the Lord to open your eyes in a new way as you seek to find rest Under His Shadow.

THE DIVINE NURTURER

My husband and I were away at a pastor's conference when I was preparing to write this chapter. While walking the streets of New York I told the Holy One, "This is a hard chapter, Lord. How can I present the Holy Spirit when I don't fully understand Him myself?" In my mind I heard Him whisper: *I am the Divine Nurturer.* I answered, "Really, God? I've never heard anyone call You that before." When I got home I searched through every verse in the Bible that mentions the Spirit of God and found that He truly is the Divine Nurturer. Why would I ever doubt His leading?

The definition of the word *nurture* is multifaceted. It usually refers to one who gives life and then feeds, protects, comforts, encourages, trains, and provides rest for his or her loved ones. The Bible reveals that the Spirit of God has all of these facets and more. Follow along with me as we catch a glimpse of the Divine Nurturer.

THE HOLY SPIRIT GIVES LIFE

El Shaddai is one of my favorite names of God in Scripture. The Hebrew word El means "mighty, power, strong."[2] The exact derivation of the word *Shaddai* is unknown, but it signifies one who nourishes, supplies, and satisfies. The first time this name was used in Scripture was when God promised Abraham, who was childless at the time, that He was choosing his family to be

His special people. As their God, He promised to nourish them and supply their needs.

This aspect of the Triune God sheds light upon the nature of the Holy Spirit, who is fully God and has all the attributes that belong to Him, including the power to create physical life. The Father, Son, and Holy Spirit miraculously created human life and everything else in the universe when the earth was formless and empty (Genesis 1:26).

Even more miraculous, the Holy Spirit is also the source of spiritual life. We are all born into the physical world, but many people get confused about the necessity and nature of spiritual birth. All of humanity is born in sin because our original parents, Adam and Eve, disobeyed God. Thankfully, when we receive Christ as our Savior, a great change is made in our hearts— something we cannot do for ourselves. We are born again spiritually and become entirely different from what we were before. The Spirit of God is the source of this second birth: "The Spirit alone gives eternal life. Human effort accomplishes nothing. And the very words I have spoken to you are spirit and life" (John 6:63).

In addition to being the source of physical and spiritual life, the Spirit of God has the power to restore emotional life. When David felt crushed beneath the weight of his troubles in Psalm 143:4-10, the Spirit of God brought stability to his emotions by leading him to level ground. He is present for all who seek Him, to those who draw near and learn to rest Under His Shadow.

THE HOLY SPIRIT FILLS US

The Bible teaches that the Holy Spirit fills believers, but this is not talking about being filled physically. Our spiritual hunger and thirst are far more extensive than our physical needs. God's Spirit fills our souls with things we can't get for ourselves—things that are impossible to attain with money, charm, wit, strength, or intellectual pursuit.

We read in Romans 5:5, "This hope will not lead to disappointment. For we know how dearly God loves us, because he has given us the Holy Spirit to fill our hearts with his love." The Greek word for love in this passage is *agape*, which means "unconditional love that is always giving and impossible to take or be a taker. It devotes total commitment to seek your highest best no matter how anyone may respond. This form of love is totally selfless and does not change whether the love given is returned or not."[3] This kind of love is unlike any we have ever known and provides healing comfort for every wound that we have experienced. It is only accessible through the power of the Holy Spirit and is revealed through Jesus' life, which was a selfless model for humankind.

God fills us with His unconditional love through the intoxicating presence of the Holy Spirit: "Don't be drunk with wine, because that will ruin your life. Instead, be filled with the Holy Spirit, singing psalms and hymns and spiritual songs among yourselves, and making music to the Lord in your hearts" (Ephesians 5:18-19). Too much alcohol can take control of a person's mind and body, resulting in slurred speech, impaired balance, loss of muscle coordination, and reduced inhibitions. Like alcohol, the filling of the Holy Spirit is exhilarating and excites us to act differently than before. He enables us to exhibit the characteristics of Christ, which is not possible in our own strength. When we surrender the control of our lives to the Holy Spirit, He can use our eyes to see as He sees, our ears to hear His voice, our hands and feet to go where He leads, and our hearts to love others the way He desires.

Being filled with the Holy Spirit is not a onetime action. It is a daily, ongoing event where we give up the control of our lives and place it in the hands of the One we can trust. While we may desire for the Spirit to control our minds continually, there are unfortunately many interruptions in this process as we daily struggle with things like gossip, envy, selfishness, unforgiveness, and many other temptations. Whenever we are enticed by the world, the flesh, or the devil, all we must do is confess it and ask for the Holy Spirit to control us once again. Sometimes this process can occur over and over, but when we relinquish control to the Holy One, we are filled with His divine presence.

We will continue to feel abandoned and empty until the Holy Spirit takes His rightful place in our lives. He nourishes our souls and fills all the empty places in our hearts with something exceedingly superior to food. This exhilarating refreshment will provide all the healing comfort we need to experience a joy-filled life.

THE HOLY SPIRIT EMPOWERS

When the Holy Spirit arrived after Christ's death and resurrection, the lives of Jesus' followers were dramatically altered. Many of them had known Jesus personally, but after they received the Spirit of God they were totally transformed. This acute awareness of God's abiding companionship continued throughout their lives as the Holy Spirit supernaturally empowered them to do things that were impossible without Him.

Human language is inadequate to express who our eternal God is, so we need His divine assistance. Like the early believers, we can experience supernatural understanding concerning spiritual things because the power of the Holy Spirit enlightens us. Jesus promised the first-century believers that they would receive power from heaven to help them understand these mysteries (John 16:13).

This same promise is true for us today. The Bible can be merely words on a page that we store in our minds, or it can be life-giving revelation if we allow the Spirit to speak directly to our hearts. He can take the mysteries of God and translate them into something that we can understand and apply.

The power of the Holy Spirit is also liberating. Paul communicated this to the believers in Rome: "So now there is no condemnation for those who belong to Christ Jesus. And because you belong to him, the power of the life-giving Spirit has freed you from the power of sin that leads to death" (Romans 8:1-2). The word *freed* in this passage means set free from the dominion of sin. This means that the Holy Spirit can liberate us from the voices that try to woo us away from our Beloved. But how do we access this power?

We are filled with the Holy Spirit when we accept Christ as our Savior, but many times we don't know how to access His power. This reminds me of a story my dear friend Bernadette Musakura once told me. Bernadette grew up in a small village in Rwanda where she lived in a hut that had no electricity or running water. Then she had the opportunity to go to boarding school for high school:

> Switching on and off the light was a new challenge for
> me. I had learned about something called electricity
> in primary school but had never seen it with my own
> eyes. The first night in high school, I didn't know how
> to get the light on so I went to bed in the darkness.
> But the following day I mastered how to switch it on
> and off, and I enjoyed being able to see clearly for the
> first time without using firewood, or the moon and
> the stars.

Like Bernadette and electricity, many of us know about the power of the Holy Spirit but don't know how to access it. Being filled with this divine power requires more than simply flipping a switch to the correct position. We must surrender the control of our lives in order for His power to become unleashed in us. I sometimes argue: "I don't want to give You control because I'm afraid of where You might lead me, or I wonder if You'll keep me safe." But even though it was scary at first, I now desire to give the Holy Spirit permission to control me each morning and then continually throughout the day. There are many times when I take over, but the Holy One patiently waits for me to allow Him to take control of the wheel again. The journey is much smoother when He's doing the driving.

Pam was surprised by the transforming power of the Holy Spirit when she handed over control:

My life was pretty ordinary until several years ago when I met a woman who often came into my retail business. Most of our talks revolved around our spiritual beliefs, and I recognized that there was something different about her. I tried to convince her (and myself) that I was content with my faith, but deep down inside I knew that something was missing. Sometimes she prayed for me, and it was powerful. She prayed about things that I hadn't told her, and yet, surprisingly, she knew what to say. When I asked how this happened she said something that I didn't understand: that she allowed the Holy Spirit to empower her.

My family began to struggle with health problems at the same time my business was failing. Each day seemed to bring more bad news, and in time I became disappointed with life. I told the Lord, "You promised an abundant life, but that's not what I'm experiencing. This can't be all there is."

I remembered what my friend said and asked the Holy Spirit to take over. Suddenly, I felt power surging through me. I was frightened at first, but in time I found that the more time I spend with Him, the more I trust Him. The trials in my life didn't suddenly disappear, but I have peace when He is in control.

You can experience the amazing power of the Holy Spirit when you give Him control. Then you will find the life-changing power needed for healing.

THE HOLY SPIRIT HELPS

Aware of the approaching hour of His death, Jesus warned His disciples that He would soon be leaving them. Naturally, they became anxious and afraid in response to what seemed like tragic news. For three years they had found comfort in His presence, and even though they hadn't always understood who He was or what He was all about, they had sensed that the gap between heaven and earth had somehow been bridged by this Man. Recognizing the fear in their hearts, Jesus was moved to make a tender promise to His beloved disciples:

> I will ask the Father, and He will give you another
> Helper, that He may be with you forever; that is the
> Spirit of truth, whom the world cannot receive, because
> it does not see Him or know Him, but you know Him
> because He abides with you and will be in you. I will
> not leave you as orphans; I will come to you.
>
> JOHN 14:16-18, NASB

The Good Shepherd lovingly promised that He wasn't leaving them as lost and comfortless sheep. He assured them that He would manifest Himself to them in a new and different way. This meant that the Spirit would graciously care for them in the same way that Jesus had.

The word *helper* in the Greek means "one who is called to someone's aid."[4] It has an even deeper implication of someone who gives help in times of distressing need or difficulty. There are times when I feel lonely and afraid as I did as a small child and I wish that Jesus could be with me in human form as He was with

His disciples. Begging Jesus to please be with me, I sometimes forget the very important fact that the Holy Spirit is "in me." He is not here to take away my trials, but to help me through them.

Jesus' promise to His fearful children in John 14 is also true for you and me today. The Helper will be in us always, standing by to love, comfort, and protect. Our part is simply to recognize His presence and call upon Him in faith. Once this truth gets firmly embedded in our hearts and minds, we will no longer feel afraid, lonely, hopeless, or inadequate.

THE HOLY SPIRIT COMFORTS

The Bible teaches that the Spirit of God brings comfort in times of distress. The early church experienced this divine comfort: "The church throughout all Judea and Galilee and Samaria enjoyed peace, being built up; and going on in the fear of the Lord and in the comfort of the Holy Spirit, it continued to increase" (Acts 9:31, NASB).

I was in desperate need of this kind of comfort because of my mother's emotional abandonment. The evil one used this pain to prevent me from believing that any mother could want me, so even though God gave me a few precious women who tried to nurture me, I couldn't receive their love. My gaping mother wound was so deep that no person could soothe it.

I had heard that God could comfort me like a mother, but I couldn't comprehend it. The words that God spoke through the prophet Isaiah were confusing to me:

> Thus says the LORD, "Behold, I extend peace to her
>   like a river,
> And the glory of the nations like an overflowing stream;
> And you will be nursed, you will be carried on the hip
>   and fondled on the knees.
> As one whom his mother comforts, so I will comfort you.

And you will be comforted in Jerusalem."
Then you will see this, and your heart will be glad.
ISAIAH 66:12-14, NASB

These verses promise that we can find comfort in the Holy One, yet many times we disregard the presence of the Holy Spirit in our lives and choose to work out our problems on our own. Hannah Whitall Smith, who experienced great pain in life, wrote, "It is pure and simple unbelief that is at the bottom of all our lack of comfort, and absolutely nothing else. God comforts us on every side, but we simply do not believe His words of comfort."[5]

When we grow to trust the Spirit of God, we can nestle into Him and bask in His nurturing comfort. His healing balm will miraculously pour over our wounded souls, and we will experience healing.

THE HOLY SPIRIT GUIDES

My husband and I have the privilege of leading groups to the Holy Land with our Israeli tour guide, Erez, who knows countless historical and cultural facts. Always checking ahead to make sure that it's safe, Erez leads us on marvelous excursions and to comfortable places to eat and rest. Without him, we might still be wandering in the wilderness.

It's essential to have a dependable guide on the broken road of life, but many times we think that our plan is the best and are not willing to listen to others. You may be surprised to find that Jesus had a guide while He lived on earth: "Then Jesus, full of the Holy Spirit, returned from the Jordan River. He was led by the Spirit in the wilderness" (Luke 4:1).

As part of the Trinity, Jesus is a natural leader, but in His humanity He allowed the Spirit to guide Him. If the Messiah submitted His will to the Holy Spirit, how much more important is it for us to do the same? The Spirit of God is the true source of understanding, but we must have an intimate relationship with Him before we can trust Him to lead. This requires heartfelt communication.

We can read the Bible over and over again, but unless the Holy Spirit softens our hearts, all we'll see are words on a page. The Spirit makes our ears sensitive to the voice of God. We must sit at God's feet with our Bibles open each day. As our hearts soften in worship and our hands open wide, we are ready to receive all that the Holy One has for us. If our ears are alert we can catch the Holy Spirit's gentle whispers beckoning us into the place of healing, where we find freedom from the powers of darkness that harden our hearts toward God.

When the Holy Spirit is our guide, we don't need to be afraid. He will give us all we need in tough situations. We can find safety as we trust Him to direct our every step on the broken road.

THE HOLY SPIRIT GIVES JOY

A shift occurs in the New Testament between the four Gospels and the book of Acts. The mood is subdued in the Gospels, but the arrival of the Holy Spirit at Pentecost brings an obvious change in the emotional tone: "The believers were filled with joy and with the Holy Spirit" (Acts 13:52). Deep, heartfelt joy like this cannot be created or experienced from anything in our physical world—it is a gift from the Holy Spirit and does not depend on circumstances.

Christ was constantly under the critical eye of the religious leaders, yet He was filled with the joy of the Holy Spirit (Luke 10:21). Amazingly, we can be filled with this same joy no matter what our circumstances are. When we remember that the Holy Spirit is always with us, nothing can steal this heavenly joy.

So how do we attain this kind of ecstasy? I find supernatural joy in worship. Even when my circumstances are harsh, I turn my eyes to the Holy One and He fills me with His joy. Satan cannot steal this kind of joy because it is eternal.

THE HOLY SPIRIT PRAYS

One of the most nurturing aspects of the Holy Spirit is His loving concern for us expressed in intercessory prayer to the Father. He knows our every need and makes petitions for us, just as loving parents do for their children (Romans 8:26).

Sometimes I am so upset and confused that I don't know what to pray. In those times I am grateful to know that the Spirit of God is interceding for me. He knows exactly what to say because He knows my innermost needs. I am able to rest Under His Shadow because the Holy Spirit cares enough to make petitions to the Father on my behalf.

FINDING REST

When the Holy One revealed Himself as my Divine Nurturer, I experienced a major breakthrough in my healing journey. I found the comforting heart of my Beloved and was able to experience divine peace for the first time.

While I was writing this chapter, my fifty-year-old brother-in-law was involved in a motorcycle accident. As the medical team tried to stabilize him for surgery, our family and friends prayed without ceasing, trusting that God would help him survive. When we received the call that he didn't make it, I was stunned. Facing a funeral that came too soon, I just wanted to be held.

Thankfully, I am intimately acquainted with my Divine Nurturer and can pour out my grief to Him. He comforts me with His loving presence, and I am no longer lonely and afraid. I am able to return to joy as He holds me. It doesn't matter what I have before me when the Holy One is hovering over me. This is what it means to find rest Under His Shadow.

Perhaps your mother provided the comfort you needed to return to joy when you were a child, but no human being is without flaw. There are times when even the utmost attempt at human nurturing is not enough. The Holy Spirit is the Divine

Nurturer who loves you with an everlasting love. When you rest
Under His Shadow, you will find healing for every mother wound
that you have sustained. I can say this with authority because I
am experiencing it in my own life. My prayer for you, dear one,
is that you will experience the healing comfort of the Holy Spirit.

> May the LORD, the God of Israel, under whose wings you
> have come to take refuge, reward you fully.   RUTH 2:12

UNDER HIS SHADOW STUDY

DAY 1: THE DIVINE NURTURER

1. Jill Briscoe found that being Under His Shadow was like a "warm, comforting heavenly blanket." Read Psalm 57:1 and Psalm 61:2-4 and describe the picture that comes to your mind when you think about resting Under His Shadow.

2. Like many people, I had been mistaken about the Holy Spirit for most of my spiritual life. Explain how you have viewed this mysterious person of the Trinity before reading this chapter.

3. What does Romans 10:17 say about faith? Describe the many ways that you personally hear and interact with the Word of God. Which kind of interaction affects you most deeply?

4. What do Romans 8:11 and John 6:63 say about the involvement of the Holy Spirit in the life-giving process? What does this mean to you personally?

5. What do you think Jesus meant in John 3:1-7 when He told Nicodemus that "the Holy Spirit gives birth to spiritual life"? Have you received this gift from the Holy Spirit? If so, how has it changed your life? If not, is it something you would like to have?

6. Worship the Holy One and ask Him to help you believe what you already know about the Holy Spirit. Record your thoughts here or in a journal. (Optional worship verses: Psalm 5:11-12.)

DAY 2: THE HOLY SPIRIT FILLS US

1. Read Ephesians 5:18-21 and explain these verses so that a child can understand.

2. How has your life changed as a result of being filled with the Holy Spirit?

3. What do you think Psalm 131:2 means?

4. Have you found quiet rest Under His Shadow, as Psalm 131:2 portrays it? If not, what do you need to do?

5. Read the prayer in Ephesians 3:14-16. What did Paul pray for the Ephesians? What do you think this means?

6. Read John 14:17 and John 15:26. What is the Holy Spirit's part in your journey to truth? Have you seen this power displayed in your life? If so, give an example.

7. What was the prophecy that Jesus said was fulfilled in Luke 4:15-21?

8. Have you experienced this kind of liberating power from the Holy Spirit? Explain your answer here.

9. Take time to ask the Holy Spirit what you need to surrender to His control. Worship the Holy One by bowing your burden at His feet. Write about it here or in a journal. (Optional worship verses: Psalm 92:1-4.)

DAY 3: THE HOLY SPIRIT HELPS

1. Read John 14:16-18. Make a list of all the ways Jesus says the Holy Spirit will help us.

2. Picture yourself there with Jesus in John 14:16-18. What would your response be to His promise?

3. Read Psalm 63:6-8. Write these verses so that a child can understand. How does this passage affect your thoughts about God?

4. Have you ever longed to be comforted but no one was available? Describe what happened and how you felt.

5. What solution does Psalm 41:3 give for this problem? Read this verse in the New Living Translation if possible.

6. Read Acts 9:31 and Psalm 119:76. How does the Holy Spirit comfort or encourage you?

7. Isaiah 66:12-14 was written to Israel but can be applied to us today as God's chosen people. Read it and personalize it here.

8. Is this truth hard for you to believe and accept? Explain your answer.

9. Read Isaiah 49:15-16 and worship the Holy One for being your Divine Comforter. Record your thoughts here or in a journal.

DAY 4: THE HOLY SPIRIT GUIDES

1. What does Jesus' example in Luke 4:1 and 4:14 reveal about our need for the Holy Spirit? How does this affect the way you view the Holy Spirit?

2. Read Psalm 32:8, John 14:17, and Romans 8:14. What do these verses say about the leading of the Holy Spirit? How does this truth affect your life?

3. God doesn't want to guide us from a distance, as if we are animals that have to be forced to follow. He wants us to draw near to His heart and allow Him to direct us from a place of sweet communion. Read Psalm 32:8-9 and describe what are you doing (or need to do) to draw near to His heart.

4. Read Romans 14:17. Describe what joy looks and feels like to you.

5. How did Paul and Silas respond to their suffering in Acts 16:24-25? Why do you think they were able to respond in this way? What can we learn from this unnatural response?

6. Spend time in worship and listen to the voice of the Holy One. Record your thoughts here or in a journal. (Optional worship verses: Psalm 16:5-9.)

DAY 5: FINDING REST

1. Read Romans 8:26-27 and paraphrase these verses in your own words. Take a few moments to reflect on the fact that the Holy Spirit has intimate knowledge of your needs and a consuming longing to meet them. How does this affect your relationship with Him?

2. Read Romans 8:6. What are you being controlled by and how is this choice influencing you? Are you satisfied or do you want to make a change? Explain your answer.

3. Read Psalm 17:8 and Psalm 36:7. List the benefits of abiding Under His Shadow that are described in these verses.

4. What is the key to finding rest according to Exodus 33:14? Are you experiencing this kind of rest? If not, what do you need to do to find it?

5. List the things that we are promised through the Holy Spirit in 1 Corinthians 2:10-16.

6. How do these promises help you find rest?

7. Spend time worshiping the Holy One and record your
   thoughts here or in a journal. (Optional worship verses:
   Psalm 36:5-10.)

CHAPTER 7

THE SHADOW OF DARKNESS

HAVE YOU EVER TRIED to do something in the dark and ended up making a big mess? One night when Gary and I were celebrating our twentieth anniversary in Italy, I got into the hotel room to freshen up . . . and couldn't get the lights on. I didn't know where Gary was until I heard his voice through the open window. I called out to him, "It's dark in here!" This was meant to be a polite hint for him to come up with our key so that I could turn the electricity on . . . but he didn't get it. Being the social guy that he is, he continued his conversation with his new friends. I tried putting on some makeup in the dark before I finally went to get the key myself. When I got back to the room I turned on the lights and looked in the mirror. Much to my horror, my reflection revealed that I had lined my lips with black eyeliner! I'm still wondering what Gary's new friends thought about my gothic look.

Like my botched makeup job, many things are done in darkness with hopes that they will never be exposed in the light. I have had the opportunity to travel all over the world and have seen the fingerprints of darkness every place I go. These are the fingerprints of Satan, who is also known as "the evil one" in Scripture (Matthew 13:19). The evil one desires to confine us in darkness.

Many people who have grown up in loving families have the same discouraging messages echoing in their minds as those who have been rejected and abused. *If people really know me, they will hate me. Nobody cares about me because I'm a loser. I need to protect myself because everyone will hurt me.* Satan uses different methods to shoot fiery darts as lies to secretly penetrate the hearts and minds of God's children. This shouldn't startle us because he has been doing this since the beginning of creation. The biblical reason for this struggle can be found when you walk through the Shadow of Darkness: "He brought them out of darkness and the shadow of death and broke their bands apart" (Psalm 107:14, NASB).

Perhaps you are thinking, *I don't want to go to a place of darkness, so let's just skip this chapter and go to the next.* Even though it would be nice to put Satan in a tidy box and try our best to ignore him, no matter how hard we try, it is impossible to contain him. Battling the evil one is an unsettling topic, but we need to understand that while we may never initiate spiritual warfare, Satan has initiated warfare against us. Therefore, we must always be armed and ready for battle . . . because it will come.

THE RESULTS OF THE FALL

The world was overtaken by darkness when Satan waged war against humankind, beginning with Adam and Eve. They had enjoyed intimate fellowship with their Creator, who allowed them to eat from any tree in the garden—except one. Theirs was an overflowing cup of blessing, but Satan lured them to believe that they needed something more to be happy. He persuaded them to believe that God's heart wasn't for their good, and in a moment that resulted in horrific consequences, they chose to listen to this lie.

God's heart was broken as He watched innocence being replaced with shame and joy replaced with sorrow. Instead of running to their King for guidance and protection, Adam and Eve now hid from Him. But the most heart-wrenching consequence of this turn of events was that all of humankind would now be born into the world as spiritual "dead men walking" (see Ephesians 2:1-2).

Spiritual death means separation from fellowship with God. When Adam and Eve rebelled, they were sentenced to live in spiritual darkness. Since that time, all humans have become citizens of this world that fiercely opposes anything to do with God.

Satan had no idea the lengths to which the Creator would go to rescue His children. Although we were undeserving, God sent His Son to die on the cross to pay the required price for our sins. This disarmed and dethroned Satan, and as a result, those who believe in Christ have been reconciled to God. As believers, we have the upper hand in spiritual warfare, but victory does not come automatically. The devil will not surrender one inch of ground unless he is forced to. He uses guerrilla warfare tactics such as trickery, deception, intimidation, and fear to keep us in bondage. He tries to trick us into believing that God is not trustworthy and that we need something other than Him to be happy. If he can gain control of our thoughts and make us believe his nasty lies, we will remain in spiritual darkness.

Over the years I have felt confused about how to fight practically against the forces of darkness. I recognized that Jesus died so that all believers, including me, could have victory over the evil one, but as I walked through the Shadow of Darkness, I learned that we have an important role to play. While God has provided the keys to freedom, He will never force anyone to use them. Victory is possible only by using military tactics to outmaneuver and aggressively resist the enemy.

KNOW WHO THE ENEMY IS

One of the key things in a battle is to know who the enemy is. Many times we think the person we are struggling with is our adversary. We must remember this important biblical truth: "We are not fighting against flesh-and-blood enemies, but against evil rulers and authorities of the unseen world, against mighty powers in this dark world, and against evil spirits in the heavenly places" (Ephesians 6:12). Who are these mighty powers of darkness? They are Satan and his evil demonic allies.

God desires for us to draw near and walk in His light, but He will never force us. Satan, on the other hand, has no problem with trickery, manipulation, or whatever it takes to control us. He is known in the Bible by many names, including Lucifer, the devil, the prince of this world, the adversary, the father of lies, and the accuser. Second Corinthians 2:11 tells us that he is also a schemer. Author Quinn Schipper describes Satan this way: "The devil is unrelenting in his work to deceive, disunite, and destroy. In whatever way relational separation occurs, this nemesis capitalizes on every opportunity to keep people divided within themselves, from others, and from their Creator."[1]

Before His betrayal Jesus warned His disciples, "I have told you all this so that you may have peace in me. Here on earth you will have many trials and sorrows. But take heart, because I have overcome the world" (John 16:33). Even though we have been warned to expect trials, many people are quick to rail at God when things go wrong. We reason, *I have chosen to walk with God instead of doing things that bring satisfaction to my flesh. Why shouldn't I expect Him to protect me from the harsh things in life?* This is exactly what Satan desires: to confuse us about who the real enemy is. Instead of being mad at God, the proper response in trials is to take our anger out on Satan.

Dan and Lindie Bacon were career missionaries who recognized who the enemy was during great tragedy:

Never in our wildest dreams would we have envisioned ourselves in the fire station outside the Sandy Hook Elementary School in Newtown, Connecticut, where our six-year-old granddaughter, Charlotte, and nineteen other children and six adults were senselessly killed by a mentally deranged young man. Yet on that day the frightening reality that we and twenty-five other families had just been robbed of a loved one became increasingly clear. The following days were like a slow-moving nightmare as our community sought to deal with this tragedy. Thousands of people descended upon our small town as funerals took place, including one for our beloved Charlotte.

Several months later, we visited the school where this horror occurred. We could feel the evil presence of Adam Lanza as he shot his way through the front door, seeking to kill as many people as possible. Yet even as we stood at the very spot where Charlotte's body was found, we sensed God's peace and comfort.

We've experienced terrible loss and grief, but we have also been comforted by a God who fully knows the pain of loss and separation. When asked by a TV reporter, "Where was God when this happened, and why didn't He protect the children?" I responded, "God didn't plan this event. It was the outworking of Satan through a whole set of sad and tragic circumstances coming from man's free will and choices. God has been present and at work through all of these circumstances and is using it for good."

Dan and Lindie experienced great tragedy, but the evil one has not shaken their faith. They know who the real enemy is and see that God's power is greater.

KNOW WHO THE VICTOR IS

When my mother was dying, I prayed for one last chance for her to look into my eyes and tell me that she loved me. That did not happen. In fact, she was angry with me for many reasons, most of them stemming from the healthy boundaries my counselor advised me to put into place. The evil one used this to stir up old lies about being unlovable. The same lies that had haunted me in the past began tormenting me again. I was the target of Satan's fiery darts, but he was not to be the victor because I recognized that God is the victor.

The King of kings is in control of the universe (Colossians 2:9-10). He never looks down to say, "Oops, I didn't mean for that to happen." Lucifer, however, is merely a fallen angel and is limited in what he can do to a believer, so we don't need to be afraid of him.

Too often we fear Satan because we gravely miscalculate his power. When we picture the spiritual battle in the heavenlies, we tend to believe that the good and evil forces are equally matched and that we will be defeated if we don't pray the right words or follow the correct steps. Let's not give Satan more authority in our lives than he deserves!

HOW TO TEAR DOWN STRONGHOLDS

Have you been puzzled by the fact that you are a Christian and yet you continue to experience negative feelings and devastating defeat? Like many believers, you may sometimes fall back under the influence of the evil one and live a frustrated and defeated life.

I don't believe a Christian can be possessed by a demon because "possession" denotes ownership, and those who have been bought by the blood of Christ belong to Him. However, when we agree with Satan's lies we allow his influence to dominate our thinking. This can build a stronghold in our minds against the truth of God.

Putting on the armor of God helps us combat the strongholds. The armor of God is far more than an invisible piece of protective clothing. Each item is equipped with supernatural empowerment from the Holy One:

> Put on every piece of God's armor so you will be able
> to resist the enemy in the time of evil. Then after the
> battle you will still be standing firm. Stand your ground,
> putting on the belt of truth and the body armor of God's
> righteousness. For shoes, put on the peace that comes
> from the Good News so that you will be fully prepared.
> In addition to all of these, hold up the shield of faith
> to stop the fiery arrows of the devil. Put on salvation as
> your helmet, and take the sword of the Spirit, which is
> the word of God.   EPHESIANS 6:13-17

Tearing down strongholds begins with true repentance and becoming right with God. True repentance isn't just feeling remorseful because you are caught doing something wrong. Rather, your heart is broken because the Holy One has revealed your sinful behavior—and you turn away from it. When you bring that which is in the darkness into the light, the power that the evil one has over it is broken.

To overcome Satan's condemning lies, we must confess our sins and put on the vital piece of armor that covers our heart: *the breastplate of righteousness*. If we go into battle without this important piece of armor, we will be knocked to the ground in defeat. Amazingly, our righteousness is secure in Jesus because of what He accomplished on the cross. I love the way that the apostle Paul put it: "We faithfully preach the truth. God's power is working in us. We use the weapons of righteousness in the right hand for attack and the left hand for defense" (2 Corinthians 6:7). When we use the weapons of righteousness, we are well equipped for both offensive and defensive battles against the forces of darkness.

We can also use the Word of God to tear down strongholds. When I'm struggling with wrong thoughts, I get on my knees and read through certain Scriptures and speak them out loud. The words that come out of our mouths are very powerful and can break the control that the evil one is trying to hold over us. At other times I speak boldly to the evil one, by the authority of the blood of Christ, demanding that he get away from me. God's supernatural power is unleashed on my behalf when I verbally acknowledge the Scriptures as truth (Revelation 12:11).

I learned a valuable lesson about tearing down strongholds from my eighteen-month-old grandson Kase. He loved being the center of attention, so whenever he was slightly hurt he would wail loudly and sometimes hold his breath until he passed out. His parents lovingly helped him toughen up. They began to say, "Shake it off, Kase! Shake it off!" and Kase would shake his whole body until he regained his composure.

The next time I was tempted by one of Satan's lies, instead of giving in to the deception and losing my emotional balance, I spoke Scripture out loud and said to myself, "Shake it off, Bev. Shake it off!" Instead of marinating in the lies from the evil one, I began to meditate on the truth of my Beloved—and slowly a stronghold was torn down.

RECOGNIZE WE ARE NOT FIGHTING ALONE

In many battles in the Old Testament, God led Israel in a glorious victory without any help from the Israelites. Usually, however, He fought alongside them, but the victory was just as miraculous. Either way, they were always assured that they didn't need to be afraid: "Be strong and courageous! Do not be afraid or discouraged. For the LORD your God is with you wherever you go" (Joshua 1:9).

Once again, we see the important impact that these two simple words—*with me*—can have in the life of a believer. The knowledge that the almighty King is always with me, leading, guiding, and providing divine power for the battle, has changed the way I view spiritual warfare.

What do you think about when you contemplate the words *with me*? I think of "Immanuel," a name for Jesus which in Hebrew means "God is with us." It gives me great peace to know that I am not alone in the battle because Jesus, Immanuel, is with me. The psalmist understood this truth: "Even though I walk through the valley of the shadow of death, I fear no evil, for You are with me; Your rod and Your staff, they comfort me" (Psalm 23:4, NASB).

Ephesians 6:15 tells us to support our feet with *the gospel of peace*. The gospel of peace is about Immanuel, and when He is with us, the balance changes. We won't fall because our feet are secure in Him. The stronghold of Satan begins to crumble, and another stronghold takes its place—the stronghold of protection in the gospel of peace.

RECOGNIZE THE VOICE OF THE GOOD SHEPHERD

Jesus said, "My sheep listen to my voice; I know them, and they follow me" (John 10:27). As our Good Shepherd, Jesus speaks truth and will never say anything that is in opposition to what is written in the Bible. When being questioned by Pilate before His crucifixion, Jesus said, "I was born and came into the world to testify to the truth. All who love the truth recognize that what I say is true" (John 18:37). This means that Jesus is the *belt of truth* that helps us conquer Satan's deception. Therefore, it is crucial that we know the Word of God in order to recognize the voice of the Good Shepherd. Donald Miller says: "If we hear, in our inner ear, a voice saying we are failures, we are losers, we will never amount to anything, this is the voice of Satan trying to convince the bride that the groom does not love her. This is not the voice of God. God woos us with kindness."[2]

We can know God's truth in our head, but if it isn't in our heart we won't be able to use this important piece of armor effectively. So how do we recognize the voice of the Good Shepherd? One of the Greek words used for *voice* is related to a word meaning "to bring forth into the light, cause to shine, shed light." These words describe what happens when we hear the Good Shepherd's voice. His words are revealed when we read the Bible. The Holy Spirit shines His light on the Word to make the Scriptures come alive and reveal what had been previously hidden. When our minds are enlightened to the truth, the illuminated Word of God becomes a defensive *sword of the Spirit*!

The following prayer will help you discern the voice of the Good Shepherd: "If this is from the True and Living God, I accept it. If it is not, I reject it. Show me, Lord, if it is from You."[3]

RECOGNIZE CHINKS IN YOUR ARMOR

A chink is an opening in a suit of armor that creates a weak spot that can be broken through. In ancient times, this placed a soldier in battle at risk for injury and possible loss of life. We all have chinks in our spiritual armor where we are more vulnerable to demonic attack. These are the areas of weakness where we are most vulnerable to the lies of the evil one. One way a chink can be recognized is by the irrational reaction it stirs up within you. The evil one knows exactly where these chinks are, so it is important for you to become aware of them also.

From the time I was a child, I believed that no one wanted me, and as a result, the greatest chink in my armor is rejection. When someone is upset with me, or when I think they are, my mind begins to meditate on lies and negative thoughts. Whether it's real or not, the power is the same. Satan's lies can sound completely true, which makes it hard for me to determine the source. I now know that if any thought makes me feel like I am a failure, lonely, ashamed, or fearful of God or the safe people in my life, it's not from the Good Shepherd.

There is a huge difference between recognizing that you have made a mistake or feel rejected by someone and feeling like that mistake or rejection is "who you are." My husband was raised in a loving family, so he doesn't like the word *loser*. I recently asked him, "Have you ever felt like a loser?" He was silent for a minute and then replied, "Well yes, I've lost things before." Everyone has losses from time to time, but some people feel like their losses define who they are. This kind of thinking can create chinks that allow Satan to gain access and form strongholds.

What are the chinks in your armor? Do you become paralyzed with fear when you feel like you are a failure, not good enough, out of control, or rejected and abandoned? Perhaps your chink is pride, fear of the unknown, perfectionism, anger, lust, or a critical attitude. Do you allow these things to define who you are?

Paul warns, "Do not conform to the pattern of this world, but be transformed by the renewing of your mind. Then you will be able to test and approve what God's will is—his good, pleasing and perfect will" (Romans 12:2, NIV). We all have chinks that can keep us from renewing our minds with the things of God. When we recognize these weak points, we can become better equipped to fight against the evil one. When a negative thought comes to our minds, we must ask ourselves, "What aspect of the Holy One's character am I doubting? What promises of my Beloved am I rejecting?" When we do this, we can see the root of the lie and pull it up so that it can't grow.

HAVE THE PROPER ATTITUDE FOR BATTLE
In preparation for war, soldiers are trained to be strong and confident in their abilities to defend themselves and others. The Bible

teaches that in spiritual warfare the opposite attitude is necessary: "Humble yourselves before God. Resist the devil, and he will flee from you. Come close to God, and God will come close to you" (James 4:7-8). Instead of being self-sufficient, we are called to be humble and totally dependent on our Beloved.

I wasn't able to experience victory in warfare until I humbly admitted that I needed Christ to rescue me. This required getting rid of the walls I had constructed for self-protection most of my life. God wanted to protect me in the shelter of His stronghold, but as long as I was trying to protect myself, He couldn't do His job. Besides, if He allowed me to win the battle by my own effort, I would snatch the crown of victory for myself and become an even greater target for the evil one.

As I humbled myself, I put the helmet of salvation in the proper place, recognizing that Christ won the war when He died on the cross in my place. It is He, not I, who is the victor (2 Corinthians 2:14).

When you bow low before the Holy One and recognize that He is the one who saves you, He will draw you to His heart, where you can obtain supernatural strength for the battle.

USE THE WEAPON OF WORSHIP

Have you ever struggled with thoughts like *If God really loved me, He wouldn't allow this to happen to me*? Satan plants these kinds of seeds because he wants to keep us from trusting the Holy One in the midst of trials. Paul and Silas used an important weapon against the evil one when they were imprisoned in Philippi: "About midnight Paul and Silas were praying and singing hymns to God, and the other prisoners were listening to them" (Acts 16:25, NIV).

When we worship the Holy One during trials, our minds are filled with His truth, leaving no room for the lies that we have been tempted to believe. Paul Billheimer describes it in this way:

"In short, Satan is allergic to praise, so where there is massive triumphant praise, Satan is paralyzed, bound, and banished."[4] Worship is essential for our faith to grow, thereby creating a powerful shield of faith against the attacks of Satan. The truth of God protects us from Satan's fiery darts (Psalm 3:3).

There are times when my heart is broken and I don't feel like worshiping. When this occurs, I choose to fall on my knees before the Holy One even though my heart is hardened. I verbally reject the lie that tells me I am unwanted. My Beloved wants me, and His love is more than enough to fill my every longing. I worship and press into Him, choosing to embrace Him instead of fighting against the pain. I picture Jesus close beside me, never leaving me—and He gives me strength. I ask the Holy Spirit to comfort me and fill up the empty places in my heart, and He whispers the truth into my ear that gently replaces the lies of Satan.

THE LIES EXPOSED

Emerson, our four-year-old granddaughter, has three older brothers so her mother and I love to dress her in girly clothes. Recently she decided that she no longer liked pants with ruffles on the bottom. No matter how much we tried, she refused to wear them . . . at least not until her daddy told her how cute she looked in them. Her father's opinion impacted her view of frilly pants, which she now proudly wears.

As the strongholds in my life were torn down, I was able to hear my heavenly Father's voice as He spoke the truth over me. And like Emmy, it was only then that I realized that I am not defined by what I did or what people did to me. I am defined by what Christ did for me! With this knowledge, the lies began to come out of the darkness as God shed His glorious light upon them.

The lie that said *I am a detestable piece of trash* came out of the darkness as I embraced the truth. Now I know that I am precious in God's sight and am the apple of His eye. God is restoring my childlike innocence as I climb up on His lap and receive His love.

The lie that said *I am unwanted and rejected and will never belong to anyone* lost its power as I chose to believe that God has chosen me for His own and adopted me into His family. Everyone desires a place to belong, a place in the world. As I bow my pain before the Lord, He is showing me that I belong to Him and restoring fullness of life to all my broken places.

The lie that said *I can't trust God or anyone because no one protected me* shifted as I understood that God was fighting a spiritual battle for me in the heavenlies and that even though evil people hurt my body, He saved my soul for Himself. When my trust in others died, I became hypervigilant and cautious. When I allowed the Holy Spirit to shine His light upon the lie, He restored rest in my life.

The lie that said *If people really know me, they will hate me* was broken. Although I wasn't loved as a child, I am not an unlovable person. I've found that people love me more when I am real and honest about my struggles. My pain had caused me to become wild and restless on the inside, but this truth helped me to become comfortable with who I am in Christ. Now I am becoming free to be me.

The lie that said *I need to hurt myself in order to feel something* was one of the hardest ones to conquer. That's because I felt it was necessary to punish myself by shedding my own blood. The Bible teaches that the only way to overcome the evil one is by the blood of the Lamb. As I recognized the truth, that Jesus died on the cross and bore all the pain and shame for me, I realized that I don't have to hurt myself in order to feel like I am alive. When I hurt myself I am denying that Christ's death was enough.

The lie that said *I hate myself and want to die* was changed. Now I realize that I was an innocent little girl and bad people did bad things to me—but that didn't make me bad. I can experience

God right here on earth and don't have to die in order to be with Him. We can experience face-to-face intimacy now. As I have bowed the loss of hope before the Lord, He is restoring joy in my life and I am finding glorious hope in Him!

Overcoming Satan's lies may sound easy, but it's not. It will be one of the hardest things you ever do—but it's essential for healing. What lies have you believed that God wants to bring out into the light?

Michelle has experienced great pain, but she has learned to fight against the lies from the evil one:

> We met at church in the fourth grade and quickly became close friends. In time we began singing duets together in church, and by our sophomore year, our friendship had grown into young love. We spent hours talking on the phone and were together often. Although we were still in our teens, we made plans for a future together. Even though we had both pledged to remain sexually pure, we became more physical than we had planned.
>
> One night, after he sneaked into my bedroom window, things became heated. In spite of my objections, before I knew it he was on top of me. The pain was intense, but because my parents were sleeping in the next room, I began to cry softly and whispered, "No, no, please don't do this." He finally stopped and tearfully said that he was sorry. And then he left, just like that.
>
> Not only was I left with the devastation of losing my virginity, the boy I loved broke up with me the next day. To add to my shame, when I told my parents, my mom said, "How could you do this to me?" and my dad was silent. I began to believe Satan's lie that said, "You are a whore," and became deeply depressed. My youth pastor assured me that God forgave me, but Satan used words

from my mother to cause me to doubt: "That's a sin you can never take back."

Nearly a decade after the night I lost my innocence, I was being treated for depression and anxiety. I shared the incident with my counselor, and her words still echo in my mind: "Michelle, you were violated. You were raped by a person that you trusted." I was stunned because I considered rape to be a violent assault perpetrated by a stranger. With this knowledge I was finally able to believe that Jesus' blood was enough to cover everything . . . and I forgave my boyfriend and myself. There are many days when Satan still whispers lies in the darkness, but I am clinging to the promise that my God is in control. He is holding me in His arms and is safely guarding my tears.

TWO DIFFERENT VOICES

Two different voices call each of us. The voice of God speaks words of truth and life that bring freedom. The voice of the evil one speaks in the darkness with lies and accusations.

Have you ever struggled to determine whether a thought was the truth of God or a lie from the enemy of our souls? Sometimes Satan attempts to deceive us with something that sounds spiritual, like when he tempted Jesus in the wilderness:

Then the devil took him to the holy city, Jerusalem, to the highest point of the Temple, and said, "If you are the Son of God, jump off! For the Scriptures say,

'He will order his angels to protect you.
And they will hold you up with their hands
so you won't even hurt your foot on a stone.'"

Jesus responded, "The Scriptures also say, 'You must not test the LORD your God.'" MATTHEW 4:5-7

Satan likes to mix truth with error, so we shouldn't be surprised when he uses this tactic. Satan is so deceptive, it's hard at times to distinguish whether certain thoughts are from him or from God.

When I met my husband's family I found that they have a family whistle. This seemed strange at first because in my family, whistles were used to call dogs. The first time I heard the DeSalvo whistle was when we were in a large store and couldn't find Gary's sister, Joy. It seemed as though she had vanished into thin air, but not to worry. Gary's dad puckered his lips, and a loud shrill whistle sounded throughout the store. Suddenly Joy mysteriously appeared. I was embarrassed and thought, *Who whistles like that in the middle of a store?*

A few weeks later I was accidentally separated from the group at a ball game. But when I heard someone whistle loudly, I knew where to find my group. This happened time and time again until I became comfortable with the DeSalvo family whistle.

Gary's father started this tradition when the kids were young, and now all of our ears are trained to hear that familiar sound. We find great comfort when we hear it. If we are in a large crowd and hear the family whistle, we immediately start looking to see where it's coming from. The funny thing is that no one else seems to notice because their ears aren't trained to hear it.

It's the same way with these two voices trying to get our attention. We need to know the Good Shepherd intimately so that we can recognize His voice and allow Him to lead as we are walking the broken road to intimacy. We cannot recognize His voice unless we train our ears to hear Him speak. When we become trained to respond to His voice, we can bring the lies of the evil one out of the darkness and into the light. Then we can stand strong and find healing comfort in the arms of our Beloved and return to joy.

Because of God's tender mercy,
 the morning light from heaven is about to break
  upon us,
to give light to those who sit in darkness and in the
  shadow of death,
 and to guide us to the path of peace.

LUKE 1:78-79

THE SHADOW OF DARKNESS STUDY

DAY 1: THE RESULTS OF THE FALL

1. What does "the Shadow of Darkness" refer to in this chapter?

2. How have you viewed spiritual warfare in the past? Where did this view originate?

3. Where do Satan and his evil forces abide according to Jude 1:6, and what is in their future?

4. Satan tempted Adam and Eve to believe that they needed something other than God to be satisfied. Have you been tempted in this same way? Read Psalm 142:5-7 and write a prayer asking God to become your true source of joy.

5. What are some of the results of the Fall according to Romans 5:12-14? What impact has this had upon your life?

6. There is a solution for this problem. Read Colossians 2:13-15, 20. Describe what God has done for us. How has this been worked out in your life?

7. Worship the Holy One and thank Him for providing a solution for you. Record your thoughts here or in a journal. (Optional worship verses: Psalm 97:1-12.)

DAY 2: THE ENEMY AND THE VICTOR

1. Have you ever been confused about who the real enemy was when you were in a conflict? Read 1 Peter 5:8 and write it so that a child can understand. Who is your enemy? What is your response to this verse?

2. The King of kings is far more powerful than anyone or anything, including Satan and his demonic forces, who are merely fallen angels. Read Luke 4:35-36, Hebrews 1:3-14, and Ephesians 1:19-22 and explain how this knowledge affects your view of spiritual warfare.

3. Read Ephesians 6:13-17. How have you viewed the armor of God before reading this chapter?

4. How can you use the breastplate of righteousness to tear down strongholds?

5. There is a difference between godly sorrow and sadness because your sin has been discovered. Read 2 Corinthians 7:10-11, Jeremiah 3:10, and Psalm 25:7-12. Explain the difference between these two so that a child can understand.

6. What does 1 John 2:14 say about overcoming the evil one? How can you use the Word of God to tear down strongholds?

7. Read Psalm 55:16-19 and worship the One who rescues us from all strongholds. Record your thoughts here or in a journal.

DAY 3: RECOGNIZE WE ARE NOT FIGHTING ALONE

1. Deuteronomy 33:12 was written about the tribe of Benjamin, but because we are God's children it is true for us as well. Personalize this verse here. How does this truth affect you?

2. Jesus is Immanuel, "God with us," which means that the gospel of peace is about Him. What does Hebrews 2:14-18 say He did for us? How does this affect you?

3. Jesus is the belt of truth that conquers Satan's lies and deception. Read John 8:32, Colossians 2:7, and 1 John 2:4

and list some of the results of putting on the belt of truth. Are you wearing this weapon? If so, how has it changed your life?

4. The sword of the Spirit is wielded when the Spirit of God shines His light on Scripture to reveal the truth. Have you had an epiphany or "aha" moment while walking the broken road to intimacy? If so, explain what happened.

5. Read Psalm 40:1-8 and worship the Holy One, quietly listening to hear Him speak. Record your thoughts here or in a journal.

DAY 4: RECOGNIZE CHINKS IN YOUR ARMOR

1. We need to recognize the weak spots in our armor to be prepared for attacks from the rulers of darkness. Chinks are areas of vulnerability such as rejection, failure, abandonment, lack of control, pride, fear of the unknown, perfectionism, anger, lust, or a critical attitude. List the chinks in your armor and describe how you react to them and why.

2. Proverbs 23:7 says, "As he thinks within himself, so he is" (NASB). Ultimately, we are what we think deep down. How has the evil one used the chinks in your armor to influence the way you see yourself?

3. Read Isaiah 43:4, Romans 5:5, and Jeremiah 31:3. What does God say about His children? Do you believe that He feels this way about you? Explain your answer.

4. Paul had the proper attitude for battle. Read 2 Corinthians 12:6-10. Describe what you see in these verses. Are you surprised by verse 9? Is this the attitude you are embracing? If not, what do you need to do to get there?

5. Read 2 Corinthians 12:9-10 again and explain why it is necessary to have the proper attitude for battle.

6. Spend time worshiping the Holy One and record your thoughts here or in a journal. (Optional worship verses: Psalm 77:13-15.)

DAY 5: USE THE WEAPON OF WORSHIP

1. Read Psalm 89:15-18 and list the benefits of worship seen in this passage. What are you doing or what can you do to ensure these benefits in your life?

2. Worship is one of the best ways for our faith to grow, creating a powerful shield of faith against Satan and his attacks. Read Hebrews 11:1-6 and write a definition of faith so that a child can understand.

3. Read Mark 9:23 to see what Jesus said about the importance of faith. Explain how you are applying this important truth.

4. Sometimes we don't feel like using the weapon of worship when we are being bombarded with lies. If you are having a problem getting started, it is helpful to have some ammunition verses to say out loud to the enemy. Make a list of the lies that you struggle with and Scripture to combat them with. You can go back through this book and find Scripture passages that spoke to your heart. If you're meeting with a group, you can also ask your group to suggest passages.

5. Deuteronomy 30:19-20 warns that we must listen and obey the voice of the Lord in order to choose life over death. It also teaches that we are to stick to the Lord like glue, which can only happen when we know Him well. Explain how you are applying these important exhortations.

6. How has your view of spiritual warfare changed in light of this chapter?

7. Spend twenty minutes (or as many as you can) in worship and record your thoughts here or in a journal. (Optional worship verses: Psalm 89:5-13.)

CHAPTER 8

THE PLACE OF FORGIVENESS

"THIS CAN'T HAPPEN AGAIN!" my mother shrieked. I wondered silently, *What in the world are you talking about? It's New Year's Day and you're dying. Part of your family has come together hoping to create a Hallmark memory of our last holiday with you. We've all worked ferociously so that you could enjoy this time without having to do anything. Why are you so upset with me?*

I cried in confusion as my husband and I drove the six hours to our home in Texas after that perplexing goodbye. What did I do wrong? I thought the weekend was almost perfect . . . until the end. I found out later that Mom's parting words to the others were words of blessing: "I'm so glad you came. It was wonderful for all of us to be together." Even though this shouldn't have come as a surprise, I felt like a knife was being thrust into my heart.

That was the last time I saw my mother in her home. Our next time together was two weeks later when she was hospitalized and close to death. I still feel piercing pain from my mother's rejection as I remember that New Year's Day, but to be truthful, in time my sadness turned into anger. I tried hard to minimize my feelings and spiritualize my reactions. After all, a good

Christian should forgive and forget, right? But Mom had hurt me over and over, and although I tried to forgive, there was a wall of resentment in my heart. It was far easier for me to put a smile on my face and pretend that everything was fine.

Just outside Jerusalem is a hill called Calvary. This is where Jesus died in our place so that we could receive forgiveness (Luke 23:33-34). It is a border crossing, and unless you are willing to let go of unforgiveness, you cannot move forward on your healing journey.

IT'S HARD TO FORGIVE

We live in a broken world filled with broken people, and as a result, we have all been hurt or offended by someone else. The questions we need to ask ourselves are, "How have I been hurt? And when I am hurt, how do I deal with the accompanying anger?"

HOW HAVE I BEEN HURT?

One of the enemy's most cunning and effective entanglements is to manipulate us into holding on to offenses. The definition for the word *offend* is "to cause pain; to hurt."[1] The greatest consequence is not the pain of the wound itself; the danger lies in the wounded person holding on to it.

This is particularly true if the trauma occurred at a young age. The emotions of a young child are very intense, and the effects of an offense are immeasurably worse if the transgressor was a parent, a caregiver, or another close relative or friend. Any emotional, physical, or sexual abuse caused by someone who should have been trustworthy can haunt the child for decades—and even a lifetime.

As a result of my childhood wounds, when I am hurt by someone I replay it over and over again in my head. Sometimes I dwell on the incident in an effort to get to the place where the pain of being in the relationship is greater than the pain of being out of it. While I know this isn't biblical behavior, it's what has worked for me in the past. Ironically, I'm the one who is hurt by this unhealthy behavior.

When someone hurts you, it sometimes feels like you've been betrayed. The closer the intimacy level between the two parties when betrayal occurs, the greater the severity of emotional pain. As John Bevere notes, "To betray someone is the ultimate abandonment of covenant. When betrayal occurs, the relationship cannot be restored unless genuine repentance follows."[2]

There are three types of betrayal found in the Bible. The first is betrayal by an enemy. While this type of offense is upsetting, the results are the least painful of the three. The psalmist David wrote, "How long must I struggle with anguish in my soul, with sorrow in my heart every day? How long will my enemy have the upper hand?" (Psalm 13:2). David often begged God to vindicate him from the attacks of his enemies.

Christ, on the other hand, ushered in a new way of living. He taught that we should forgive our enemies and pray for them. In fact, He said that we should do even more than that:

> You have heard the law that says, "Love your neighbor"
> and hate your enemy. But I say, love your enemies! Pray for
> those who persecute you! In that way, you will be acting
> as true children of your Father in heaven. For he gives his
> sunlight to both the evil and the good, and he sends rain
> on the just and the unjust alike.   MATTHEW 5:43-45

The second type of betrayal is betrayal by a friend. Once again, we see that Jesus understood this kind of betrayal all too well. When Judas betrayed Him with a kiss, He said, "My friend, go ahead and do what you have come for" (Matthew 26:50). Jesus had lovingly poured His life into Judas, so how could Judas do such a thing? Jesus' other friends weren't much better: "Then all his disciples deserted him and ran away" (Mark 14:50). They had seen Jesus turn water into wine, heal the sick, and feed the multitudes with a few scraps of food. Surely they realized by now that He was the Promised Messiah. How could they betray Him? When He said from the cross, "Father, forgive them, for they don't know what they are doing" (Luke 23:34), I'm sure that His words, though directed at the angry crowd, spoke volumes to his devastated unfaithful allies.

The third type of betrayal is betrayal by a family member. Joseph, one of the twelve sons of Jacob, experienced this kind of devastating betrayal. His brothers were jealous of him, so they sold him into slavery. Thankfully, God spared his life and used this for the good of Israel. Joseph forgave his brothers, even though they had rejected and abandoned him (Genesis 50:20).

Any type of sinful behavior of others can become a stronghold in our lives. After growing up constantly hurt by family, I was the one caught in the trap of the evil one because I was holding on to offenses. I was entangled in one of Satan's evil schemes that Paul warned the Corinthians about: "When you forgive this man, I forgive him, too. And when I forgive whatever needs to be forgiven, I do so with Christ's authority for your benefit, so that Satan will not outsmart us. For we are familiar with his evil schemes" (2 Corinthians 2:10-11).

HOW DO I RESPOND TO HURT?

Our responses to being wounded take many different forms. When betrayal occurs in the early years of life, a child usually constructs emotional walls of protection to keep from being hurt again. As a result, all incoming information is processed through anxious patterns of reasoning that may be inaccurate. This form of self-protection can ultimately become a stronghold for the evil one, and the walls of protection become a source of isolation that keeps the person from drawing close to God and others.

Because of the abusive things that went on in my child-hood, I was programed, in a sense, to believe that others would betray me. I built an impenetrable wall around my wounds and could identify with the walls that Solomon talked about: "An offended friend is harder to win back than a fortified city. Arguments separate friends like a gate locked with bars" (Proverbs 18:19).

A fortified city had walls built around it and gates that could be locked tightly to keep out anyone who was considered a threat. We can construct similar walls to protect ourselves from being hurt by others. Refusing to deal with offenses may bring temporary relief, but it will not provide a permanent solution to the problem. Instead, resentment builds up in our souls.

Resentment is the fertile ground for toxic weeds like bitterness, rebellion, criticism, gossip, selfishness, jealousy, spitefulness, and blame. Bitterness takes root when anger toward a person builds up to form a self-protective hardened heart. Resentment is the perfect environment for bitterness to grow into an effective tool for the enemy. The book of Hebrews warns against this danger-ous harvest: "Look after each other so that none of you fails to receive the grace of God. Watch out that no poisonous root of bitterness grows up to trouble you, corrupting many" (12:15).

Poison can kill, injure, or impair an organism, which is the main goal of the evil one. The longer we hold on to an offense, the greater the chance for this deadly weed to become a stronghold.

Nothing multiplies the harvest of bitterness more quickly than unforgiveness, and nothing dissolves it faster than letting go of the wrongdoing. In fact, psychologists agree that the only cure for bitterness is forgiveness. When a plant is uprooted over and over again, the root doesn't have a chance to become strong. In the same way, if we forgive over and over again, grudges can be uprooted until the root of bitterness eventually withers and dies.

At this point you may be wondering, *Is it always wrong to feel anger toward someone?* Anger is a God-given emotion, just like joy and sorrow. Emotions are not sinful in and of themselves. It is what we do with them that can be destructive. Paul said, "Don't sin by letting anger control you" (Ephesians 4:26). This indicates that it is possible to be angry without sinning.

If in anger I react in a way that is harmful to myself or to others, my reaction is sinful. However, if I bow my pain and give it to the Holy One, asking and sometimes begging Him to help me deal with my negative emotions in a godly way, then it doesn't result in sinful behavior. When we lay down our anger as an offering to the Holy One, it becomes an extravagant gift to Him and He is well pleased.

GRAVE CONSEQUENCES

Recent studies reveal that holding on to grudges results in grave consequences. Unforgiveness can lead to mental health disorders such as anxiety, depression, and shame. Medical research has also documented the physiological changes that occur in the body when people are harboring a grudge. This includes elevation in blood pressure, worsening cardiovascular function, decrease in immune functioning, and increased susceptibility to disease. While the psychological and physical effects of unforgiveness are alarming, the spiritual consequences are far more severe.

The topic of forgiveness has been the most difficult of all for me to write about. After spending countless hours praying and studying about forgiveness, even though I had pages and pages of notes, I couldn't figure out what to do with them. Finally, as I was worshiping one evening, I had a conversation with the Holy One that went something like this:

> Bev: Abba, why has the topic of forgiveness been so
>   difficult for me to write about?
>
> Abba: Because it's of the utmost importance to Me.

Bev: But why is it so important? Is it because it helps
     the person who wounded me?

Abba: Yes, my daughter, they reap great benefits, but
      that's not the most important reason.

Bev: Well, does forgiving others benefit me . . . so that
     I can heal?

Abba: You are released from Satan's stronghold when
      you let go of an offense, but that's still not the
      main reason it's so important.

Bev: Okay. Do I release my grudge to gain Your favor?

Abba: My child, I am honored and glorified when you
      allow Me to sit in sole judgment, but no . . .
      that's not the main reason either.

Bev: But God . . . why is it so incredibly important for
     me to forgive those who have hurt me?

Abba: Forgiveness is my gift to you so that our sweet
      intimacy can be fully restored. When you forgive,
      it removes all barriers between your heart and
      Mine.

God gave His Son to die for us because He desires an intimate
relationship with us, but this doesn't mean that we will have unin-
terrupted fellowship with Him. There are many actions, including
unforgiveness, that can cause our hearts to harden, creating a barrier to intimacy with the Holy One. Jesus spoke about this in the
Sermon on the Mount: "If you forgive those who sin against you,
your heavenly Father will forgive you. But if you refuse to forgive
others, your Father will not forgive your sins" (Matthew 6:14-15).

I believe that Jesus was referring to the day-to-day cleansing we
obtain when we confess our sins in order to restore fellowship with
our heavenly Father. We cannot possibly walk with God in true

fellowship if we refuse to forgive others. But our eternal destiny is not based on whether we forgive others—the Bible clearly reveals that our salvation is forever secure because of what Christ did on the cross.

THE PERFECT EXAMPLE

Many of you have had unspeakable things done to you, but none can compare to the most despicable thing ever done to any human being in history. This was the crucifixion of the pure and spotless Lamb, Jesus Christ, at Calvary. He poured His heart out to the multitudes, healing the sick, extending compassion to the lonely, encouraging the discouraged, cleansing sinners, and teaching about the kingdom of God. He confused people but never hurt anyone intentionally—and yet He was despised, rejected, forsaken, beaten, mocked, spit upon, and nailed to a cross. Nevertheless, Jesus made the decision to count others as more important than Himself, even though they had hurt Him deeply, and He yielded His will to His Father. In doing so, He taught us how to handle our hurts: "Forgive as the Lord forgave you" (Colossians 3:13, NIV).

So how does the Lord forgive? His forgiveness is costly. Jesus described the torture He would go through in order for forgiveness to take place: "He will be handed over to the Romans, and he will be mocked, treated shamefully, and spit upon. They will flog him with a whip and kill him, but on the third day he will rise again" (Luke 18:32-33). Forgiveness is often costly, but God forgives graciously and He exhorts us to do the same (Ephesians 4:32). Like Jesus, we need to be willing to become uncomfortable if that's what it takes.

Jesus' forgiveness is also unconditional: "When you are praying, first forgive anyone you are holding a grudge against, so that your Father in heaven will forgive your sins, too" (Mark 11:25). We are not merely to forgive offenders only if they are repentant. Forgiveness, like love, must be unmerited and unconditional.

Maybe you are thinking: *Really, God? Do I have to forgive people even if they aren't sorry for what they've done? That's too hard!* God doesn't ask us to do something that He's not willing to do Himself. While hanging on the cross, Jesus took the initiative and forgave the people who were crucifying Him even though they weren't sorry. He forgave them without conditions, and though it seems impossible, we must forgive unconditionally as well.

God's forgiveness is also comprehensive: "He has removed our sins as far from us as the east is from the west" (Psalm 103:12). This means that because we are His children, He doesn't remember our sins any longer, no matter how great they are. He has totally forgiven us and washed away our sin, and as a result, we must forgive others completely.

We are never more like Christ than when we choose to forgive. My friend Emily learned this when she chose to forgive her father:

I grew up believing that my dad was almost perfect. He adored my mother, and was a loving and generous father and a highly successful businessman. He trusted Jesus to be his Savior and shared his faith with others. I loved my dad and took great comfort in knowing that he would always be there for me and my family.

When my father was diagnosed with Alzheimer's in his late seventies, my brother had to take over his finances. We were devastated to learn that Dad had secretly kept a mistress for over forty years. My first response was anger. How could he do this to us? After tearfully crying out to the Lord, I realized that Dad was not the only one who had sinned. I had sinned, also, when I put my confidence, security, and hope in my dad and trusted him to provide what only my heavenly Father could.

After Dad died, God reminded me that Jesus had paid for all of his sin. This freed me to forgive him, too, and remember all the blessings that God had given me through his life. I now have the hope of seeing him again—and he will be "perfect" in Christ.

MISCONCEPTIONS ABOUT FORGIVENESS

We need to clear up a few misconceptions about forgiveness. The first is that forgiveness means forgetting what happened. The definition of *forgive* is "to cease to feel resentment against an offender."[3] There is no mention of forgetting in that definition. We may try our best to forget what's been done to hurt us, but we can't forget the past. Both good and bad events remain forever etched in our memories.

There are two ways to remember a hurtful event. One is to ruminate on what happened, reliving it over and over again. When you choose this method, bitterness, anger, and fear multiply until they control your thoughts and actions. The other is to remember with grace by bowing your painful memories before the Holy One and allowing Him to comfort you. When burdens are laid before His feet in worship, painful memories lose their power and you can return to joy.

When you use an eraser, it doesn't make what was written any less true. It simply clears the board so that it can be used again. Likewise, forgiveness doesn't eliminate the offense, but it makes it possible for you to move out of your pain and into freedom.

Another misconception is that forgiveness means that you have to be hurt over and over again. This may stem from the discourse where Peter asked Jesus, "Lord, how often should I forgive someone who sins against me? Seven times?" and Jesus answered "seventy times seven" (see Matthew 18:21-22). This sounds like we have to remain in an abusive relationship indefinitely, but that's not what Jesus meant. The Jewish culture was all about rules, but Jesus basically told Peter that forgiveness is governed by love rather than by numbers or rules.

While it is true that forgiveness should be a reflection of our understanding of divine forgiveness, we must also remember that healthy boundaries are extremely important. Some people form codependent bonds because they are attracted to someone similar to a person who hurt them in the past. Codependency is when someone aids or enables another person's addiction, abusiveness, or irresponsibility. He or she depends on the other for emotional gratification no matter how badly the other person mistreats the codependent one.

If you are in a cycle of emotional abuse with another person, you must forgive—but you also need to change the way you relate to them. Unfortunately, unhealthy relationships are extremely hard to let go of because of the emotional highs and lows that accompany them. In order to establish healthy boundaries, you must recognize that God is the only one who can completely fill your emotional tank.

Although forgiveness doesn't mean that you must remain in a relationship where you are physically or sexually abused, it is extremely important to seek the will of the Holy One in every relationship you are involved in. There are no exact rules about forgiving others because each relationship is unique. When asked what it means to boldly love an abuser who isn't repentant, Dr. Dan B. Allender said, "There are no certain steps or techniques to loving boldly. The heart of the lover must be free (through walking the path of honesty and repentance) to imaginatively ponder what it means to give grace to the abuser. There are no short cuts, no clear and smooth paths to follow."[4]

I CAN'T, BUT HE CAN!

Forgiving others doesn't come naturally. It requires something that is foreign to human nature: humility. In order to forgive, we must look beyond our natural impulses and focus on imitating Jesus. This means surrendering our will and allowing the Holy Spirit to control our emotions.

Perhaps you feel uncomfortable when you hear the word *surrender*. Surrender makes me think of losing a war. But remember—the Holy One will never demand we do something under compulsion. Abdication—the formal relinquishment of your claims, rights, and power—may be a more accurate way of describing how we relate to the Holy Spirit in forgiveness. Forgiveness doesn't mean excusing or eliminating the consequences of an offense. Rather, it means humbly abdicating to the Lord and choosing to lay down our rights to punish them.

Simply saying "I forgive you" because that's what we're supposed to do isn't what God desires. In the parable of the unforgiving debtor Jesus said, "That's what my heavenly Father will do to you if you refuse to forgive your brothers and sisters from your heart" (Matthew 18:35). If we aren't broken by the love of God, we cannot become vulnerable and love others from our hearts. We can't truly love without being willing to be wounded and hurt by someone, which means that our hearts will probably be broken again at some point.

Sometimes the offense we carry is so unspeakable that it seems impossible to forgive. This is especially true if the transgressor was someone you trusted deeply or who is not repentant. It seems unfair to have to forgive in these circumstances. Letting go of resentment feels humanly impossible. But the apostle Paul told the believers at Philippi, "This same God who takes care of me will supply *all* your needs from his glorious riches, which have been given to us in Christ Jesus" (Philippians 4:19, emphasis added).

So how do I practically allow the Holy Spirit to help me forgive? When I've been hurt and can't imagine how I'll ever be able to forgive, I recognize that I am empty and need God's help. Next, I remember that I've let my heavenly Father down numerous times, and yet He never ceases to forgive me. Then I extend my hands into the air as if I am holding an empty cup toward heaven. I pray and ask the Holy One to open His storehouse of heavenly treasures and fill my cup with His forgiveness. In my mind I offer that same cup, which is now full of God's forgiveness, to the person who hurt me. This sounds simple, but it is extremely powerful.

Deborah found this to be true in her life:

> Forgiveness is difficult for anyone . . . but especially so for an eighteen-year-old whose family has been destroyed at the hands of a fellow classmate. That was my situation in what seems like a lifetime ago. While my family was driving home one night, we were hit head-on by a drunk driver. I was asleep in the backseat and miraculously escaped with only skin lacerations, but my father was killed instantly and my mother was critically injured. The person responsible for this unspeakable tragedy was well-known in my high school for his drinking binges. I was filled with so much anger toward him because my life would never be the same.
>
> While Mother lay in the hospital with extensive injuries, the young man never expressed his remorse for what he had done. I vowed that I would never forgive him, but Mother would have none of that. She modeled, even in extreme adversity, a life totally devoted to our Lord. She knew that forgiveness would only be possible through Him. Although it took many years, I finally allowed God to fill me with His strength so that I could forgive the unforgivable.

Forgiving those who hurt or abused you may possibly be the most difficult of all requirements on this journey, but, as Deborah found, it is possible with God's help.

Remember that when we forgive an offender, we are not saying that they don't deserve to be punished—we are merely releasing them to God. God is the only righteous judge. When we release someone to Him, it doesn't mean that we're letting them off the hook or that it doesn't matter that they hurt us. It simply means that we're not holding ourselves responsible to judge them (James 4:11-12). When I give the matter over to the only righteous judge, He steps in between me and that person and becomes my advocate.

Are you willing to lay your offenses at His feet and abdicate any perceived right to sit on His judgment seat? Leave your burden with the Holy One and walk away free.

Don't grieve God. Don't break his heart. His Holy Spirit, moving and breathing in you, is the most intimate part of your life, making you fit for himself. Don't take such a gift for granted. Make a clean break with all cutting, backbiting, profane talk. Be gentle with one another, sensitive. Forgive one another as quickly and thoroughly as God in Christ forgave you. EPHESIANS 4:30-32, MSG

THE PLACE OF FORGIVENESS STUDY

DAY 1: IT'S HARD TO FORGIVE

1. When you are hurt, how do you usually deal with the accompanying anger and bitterness?

2. Read the familiar passage in Luke 23:32-34 as if for the first time and picture this scene at Calvary in your mind. What would your reaction be toward the crowd if you were in Jesus' place?

3. Are you carrying any baggage of unforgiveness that is keeping you from moving forward in life? Explain your answer.

4. Have you developed a pattern of protecting your heart because you have been offended by someone in the past? How has this affected the way you react when you are hurt by someone in the present? Explain your answer.

DAY 2: HOW HAVE I BEEN HURT?

1. Have you ever been betrayed by an enemy? Explain what happened and how you responded. What was the result of your response?

2. God's Word explains why we can trust Him, even when we are betrayed by an enemy. First Samuel 25:29 says: "Even when you are chased by those who seek to kill you, your life is safe in the care of the LORD your God, secure in his treasure pouch! But the lives of your enemies will disappear like stones shot from a sling!" Do you believe that you are safe and secure in God's treasure pouch? Why or why not? How does this change the way you feel about forgiving an enemy?

3. Have you ever been betrayed by a friend? Explain what happened and how you responded. What was the result of your response?

4. What does Psalm 55:20-22 say you should do when a friend betrays you? How does this affect the way you should feel when you are betrayed by a friend?

5. Have you ever been betrayed by a family member or intimate friend who is like family? Explain what happened and how you responded.

6. When Jesus died on the cross, our sins were placed on His shoulders. As a result, God could not look upon Him with favor so the spotless Lamb of God felt forsaken by His Father. Read Matthew 27:45-46. How does this knowledge impact you?

7. Spend time worshiping the Holy One and record your thoughts here or in a journal. (Optional worship verses: Psalm 96:1-13.)

DAY 3: HOW DO I RESPOND TO HURT?

1. How do you respond when you are betrayed?

2. Where did this response originate?

3. According to 2 Corinthians 2:10-11, Satan outsmarts us if we refuse to forgive. How does he outsmart us?

4. Have you ever been ensnared in unforgiveness? Explain what happened. What can you do to resist the schemes of the devil that lead to a root of bitterness?

5. Use 2 Corinthians 5:18-21 to explain the main purpose for the death of Christ at Calvary.

6. What has been your understanding of God's forgiveness in the past? Did you think of it more as absolution from sin, or did you realize that the main purpose was so that we could have an intimate relationship with God? Explain your answer.

7. There are many physical and emotional consequences to unforgiveness, but what is the grave consequence of refusing to forgive discussed on pages 150–151? Were you surprised by this?

8. Read 1 John 3:18-24 and explain how forgiveness is related to intimacy with God so that a child can understand.

9. Spend time worshiping the Holy One and record your thoughts here or in a journal. (Optional worship verses: Psalm 103:1-13.)

DAY 4: THE PERFECT EXAMPLE

1. What were the aspects of perfect forgiveness listed in this chapter? How would you rate yourself in these areas? Explain your answer.

2. How should we live according to Ephesians 5:2? Does this seem like an impossible command to you? Explain your answer.

3. What are the misconceptions about forgiveness that are discussed in this chapter? Have you ever struggled with any of these? How has this affected your relationships?

4. Have you ever been in a relationship where you struggled to establish healthy boundaries? Explain what happened and what you did (or need to do) to correct it.

5. What do you think Jesus meant in Matthew 7:3-6? Does this shed biblical light on any misconceptions you have about forgiveness? Explain your answer.

6. Spend time worshiping the Holy One and record your thoughts here or in a journal. (Optional worship verses: Psalm 67.)

DAY 5: I CAN'T, BUT HE CAN!

1. The ability to replace bitterness and anger with forgiveness can happen only when we allow God to work through us. What does 1 John 4:16-17 say about this? What are you doing to apply these verses, or what do you need to do to apply them?

2. God's Word says that true forgiveness comes from the heart. What do 1 Peter 4:8 and Colossians 3:12-13 say about this?

3. What does Psalm 103:14-15 say about life? How does this change the way you feel about keeping short accounts?

4. Is there someone whom you are struggling to forgive? Read Psalm 23:5-6 and think about holding an imaginary cup as described on page 157. Next, pretend to hold your empty cup in the air and ask God to fill it with His overflowing blessings. Imagine it being filled up, and then offer it (in your mind) to your offender. Do this over and over until you are filled with "the peace of God, which surpasses all understanding" (Philippians 4:7, WEB). Describe your thoughts here.

5. Since God is our advocate, we can have confidence that He will defend us in a just manner. Read Psalm 37:5-9 and personalize it. What is your response to this encouraging news?

6. What do Romans 12:19 and James 4:12 say about revenge? Are you setting yourself up as a judge when you pronounce a guilty verdict on someone? How do you feel about this insight?

7. Read 1 Peter 2:21-23 and describe what Jesus did when He was hurt by others. How can you apply this in your life?

8. Spend time worshiping the Holy One and record your thoughts here or in a journal. (Optional worship verse: Psalm 28:7.)

CHAPTER 9

THE GARDEN OF GETHSEMANE

I LOVE TO PLAY Hide and Seek with my grandchildren. Hudson is a master hider and can evade his seekers by becoming quiet and still like a little mouse. Jackson, Greyson, and Emerson, on the other hand, giggle loudly and jump out from their hiding place as soon as someone comes near.

Some of us spend a lifetime playing our own version of Hide and Seek. As adults, we believe Satan's lie that says we need to protect ourselves from being hurt. We feel like we need to be strong, so we put a smile on our faces and hide our true selves from others. We become skilled at deflecting, hoping to hide ourselves away. We believe the lie that says, *If people really know me, they will hate me.*

Fortunately, God didn't create us to hide. Even Jesus, who is fully God and fully man, found solace in the companionship of His close friends. On the most challenging evening of His earthly life, the night of His betrayal, Jesus went to the garden of Gethsemane to pray: "He [Jesus] took Peter, James, and John with him, and he became deeply troubled and distressed. He told them, 'My soul is crushed with grief to the point of death. Stay here and keep watch with me'" (Mark 14:33-34).

Why did the Lord request these men to accompany Him on that dark night? On the hardest evening of His earthly life, Jesus found comfort in a few safe people. Peter, James, and John had become a safe base for Him.

Journey with me to the garden of Gethsemane, where there is no need to hide.

HIDING PLACES

God created us to live in holy interdependence with one another, where we can experience safety on home base. This is the place where we recognize one another's strengths and weaknesses and work together to fill in gaps.

If only it were that easy! We live in a sinful world where wounded people wound others. As a result of relational struggles, all of us seek hiding places.

A great strain was placed on relationships when Adam and Eve chose to go their own way in the Garden of Eden. They decided to live for themselves when they chose to believe that God was not enough to satisfy all their needs. In their fear and shame, they played the first game of Hide and Seek. They hid from the One with whom they had formerly experienced deep intimacy. Even though they were not alone, they were lonely.

Most of us have felt lonely at some point in our lives. Loneliness is different from being alone. It is not the absence of faces; it's the absence of intimacy. We can be surrounded by people but still feel lonely.

There are countless books, sermons, articles, and conferences with insightful solutions to relational difficulties, and yet we live in a time when relationships are more fractured and scattered than ever. Christians squabble over the type of teaching and music styles and even the way their church is decorated. Singles and young families live far away from the support of their extended families, fostering isolation and loneliness.

Thankfully, God has a solution. Since the fall of man He has been at work restoring relational order. Because of what Christ did on the cross, relationships that were once separated can be rebuilt through Him. This restoration is intended to be experienced in community. Jesus said that the love between believers can be one of the greatest ways to reveal the original, extravagant love of God to the world (John 13:35).

If our understanding of God is merely head knowledge, our moods can be swayed by how other people respond to us. But as we learn to grow in our understanding of God's unconditional love and experience an intimate relationship with Him, we find that He is big enough to fill every single one of our emotional needs. Then we can come out of our hiding places because we are no longer fearful of being rejected.

THE GREAT COMMANDMENTS

One day Jesus was asked by the Jewish leaders: "Of all the commandments, which is the most important?" He answered: "'You must love the LORD your God with all your heart, all your soul, all your mind, and all your strength.' The second is equally important: 'Love your neighbor as yourself.' No other commandment is greater than these" (Mark 12:28, 30-31). Why did Jesus include the second greatest commandment in His answer? I believe it's because the two go hand in hand. Mike Mason says, "No one can be close to God without also being close to people."[1]

Understanding and applying the greatest commandment has been a huge part of my healing journey. In order to truly love the Lord with all my heart, mind, and soul I had to get over my fear and misconceptions about Him. When I recognized, as if for the first time, that He loves me extravagantly, I could hardly contain my emotions for Him. When I chose to bask in His relentless desire for me, I was undone. Notice that I had a choice to make. Although I drew near to the Lord in fear and trembling, gradually emotional love for Him began to burst forth in me. But when I was honest, I had to admit that I was extremely uncomfortable with the command to love others as I love myself. In order to do this I would have to become vulnerable and risk being rejected again.

There are five levels of communication that determine the depth of intimacy we can experience in relationships. In the first level, we share simple clichés (e.g., "How is the weather?" or "It's a great day"). This is how we communicate with mere acquaintances. We can easily hide behind a mask here because conversation stays in the safe zone.

In the second level of communication, we share simple facts with others (e.g., "I had a sandwich for lunch today" or "I went to my daughter's house yesterday"). This shallow depth of intimacy allows people to stay in a nice hiding place. Texting and other forms of tech communication lend themselves to this form of "friendship lite." Unfortunately, most relationships stay at this safe place where there are no risks involved.

In the third level of communication, we share beliefs, thoughts, ideas, and opinions. We often fear getting too close or too involved in this level because we may be "found out" for who we really are. Those brave enough to venture into this unsafe zone are taking a risk that could lead to rejection and loss. In this place, most people quickly revert back to level one or two.

In the fourth level of communication, we share emotions, feelings, experiences, and what we truly feel and think. This level is rarely reached because so few people are in touch with their deepest thoughts and feelings. They have denied, medicated, or swept them under a rug for self-protection.

In the fifth level of communication, we are completely vulnerable with others. Honesty, gut-level sharing, openness, and mutual brokenness occur here. This is the most risky of all levels: the place where you are "fully known." Even so, this is where you are free to come out of your hiding place and remove all masks because you are safe. Jesus lived His life at this level of relationship and desires this kind of oneness with us. Total acceptance, overwhelming fulfillment, and the comfort needed for healing can only be experienced in this raw level of intimacy.

Because of the trauma from my childhood, I had a highly sensitive "rejection antenna" that kept me from going past the safer levels of communication. Whenever I rarely took the chance of going deeper with someone, I quickly retreated in fear. I very cautiously lived by the saying, "Hurt me once, shame on you. Hurt me twice, shame on me." This caused me to fall hook, line, and sinker for a spiritually sounding half-truth: "I can trust God and God alone." It was a lie that looked good on the outside, that I'd convinced myself was scriptural, but it was destroying something inside me. There was no way for me to trust God fully when my heart was hardened toward the people that He brought into my life.

Something needed to change in order for me to become real with others. I asked the Holy One for help and He showed me the secret to loving others. It was a new commandment that Jesus gave His disciples—a challenge for all of us to come out of our secret hiding places and enter into the deepest level of communication.

A NEW COMMANDMENT

Knowing that He was going to die soon, Jesus brought His best friends together for some important last words. For three years He had faithfully explained God's past commands, but now He had something new for them. This teaching would be essential for the unity of the church and the spreading of the gospel in His leave of absence: "So now I am giving you a new commandment: Love each other. Just as I have loved you, you should love each other" (John 13:34).

This new commandment sounds a lot like the second greatest commandment, but it calls for something radically different. Instead of simply loving others as we love ourselves, we are given a higher calling: to love others with a deeper, more intimate love that mimics Christ's love. This requires moving into the deepest level of communication.

Perhaps you are thinking, *It's hard enough for me to love others as I love myself, but it's utterly impossible to love them as Jesus does. He sacrificed His very life for the world. How could I possibly cultivate that kind of love?* Thankfully, the Holy One is in the business of transformation.

Loving like Jesus doesn't happen by following a set of rules or learning certain techniques. There is nothing we can humanly do to force this kind of divine love to grow. It can only flow forth when we open our hearts fully to the Holy Spirit.

As we move forward on the broken road and allow the Holy Spirit to control our thoughts and actions, we will see that God desires for us to enjoy relationships of all kinds. Out of the depth of intimacy with Him, He gives us a longing to relate to other people.

Cynthia Heald writes about this in her book *Becoming a Woman Who Loves.*

The Father spoke: *My child, do you know that I love you?*

Yes, Father, I know that You love me.

How do you know of My love?

You sent Your Son to die on the cross for my sins. You adopted me as Your own child. You have given me Your Holy Spirit, who has transformed my heart with your love.

Since you freely received My love, do you freely love others?

I try, Father, but I do not love perfectly.

*My child, I want you to be intent on learning to love as
I love you. It is of paramount importance to Me.*

Yes, Father. I want to do only what You desire. Here is
my heart—it is Yours. Fill it with Your love and do what
is necessary to teach me to love.[2]

Thankfully, this new kind of love doesn't depend on us. Paul
taught the Philippians that Christ would give him the strength
to do all things (Philippians 4:13). This is true for us as well.
He empowers us to love others in a divine way. No matter how
hard we try, our love will be impotent until we choose to accept,
instead of resist, the Holy One's unconditional love. When we
reject Satan's lies, the power that the evil one has over us is
broken. Only then can Christ's love flow freely through us to
others.

We cannot allow God's love to flow through us as long as we
have our protective walls in place. When we come out of hiding,
we'll find that we can be a safe place to others and find healing
comfort and joy in relationships.

THE RISKS

This new kind of love requires connecting with others, even
though there are risks involved. One day I was wrestling with
God about these risks. Our discourse went like this:

> Bev: Abba, why can't You zap me and heal me
>   miraculously?
>
> Abba: I can, but I have a better way.
>
> Bev: I know, but why can't You heal me without
>   anyone else?

Abba: Do you trust Me?

Bev: I think I do.

Abba: Then let's do it My way.

Bev: But Your way means I have to love with passion, and that hurts too much!

Abba: Yes, the love that I desire for you is risky. Jesus loved others with passion and He was rejected . . . but He kept on loving anyway.

We are called to be mirrors through which God reveals Himself to others, but every mirror is marred in some way. Every relationship in your life will disappoint you at times. People will inevitably hurt you, either accidentally or intentionally. Even good parents, spouses, relatives, and friends make mistakes and cannot possibly fill in all the gaps that are missing in our lives. Jesus is the only human who ever walked this earth without sinning, and as a human being even He couldn't meet the needs of everyone who wanted Him.

We see this in Luke 4. The crowds wanted to be with Jesus constantly because they were amazed by His teaching and authority over demons and disease. But "when day came, Jesus left and went to a secluded place; and the crowds were searching for Him, and came to Him and tried to keep Him from going away from them. But He said to them, 'I must preach the kingdom of God to the other cities also, for I was sent for this purpose'" (Luke 4:42-43, NASB). Even though it meant that some were disappointed, Jesus chose to do His Father's will.

If you have been deeply hurt in the past, don't expect to have one big breakthrough that will suddenly clear away all doubt and fear. Relational patterns can be broken in time, but it is usually a gradual change that requires seeing Jesus in others and choosing to believe that He is in control of the relationship.

SURPRISED BY THE REFLECTION

God expressed His love for us by sending Jesus to die for our sins so that we could have a second chance. No matter what kind of mess we've made of our relationships, we can start over and make things right.

As believers, we are one with Jesus and can have divine fellowship with Him and with one another. As a result, when we use our spiritual eyes to look into the hearts of our loved ones, we will be surprised by the reflection—we will see the face of Christ:

> I pray that they will all be one, just as you and I are one—
> as you are in me, Father, and I am in you. And may they
> be in us so that the world will believe you sent me.
>   I have given them the glory you gave me, so they may
> be one as we are one. I am in them and you are in me.
> May they experience such perfect unity that the world
> will know that you sent me and that you love them as
> much as you love me.   JOHN 17:21-23

This means that if Christ is in us, the magnificent glory of God dwells in us. We can see His glory in other people and learn to love them in a way that is selfless and holy. It is only in this environment that people can be healed, renewed, and restored.

Enjoying God's presence in others promotes relationships that will last. We can be present for others and focus on who they are when we remember that the Holy One dwells in them. When we see people the way that Jesus sees them, we will be able to go beyond the exterior and look into their hearts.

Laurey, the daughter of my mentally ill older sister, discovered the beauty of being seen as Jesus sees her:

> My family lived in a small town when I was a child, and
> our home was frightening and unstable. I rode to church

on the church bus because, although my parents were
Christians, they didn't take me to church. I loved going
to church and hearing about Jesus. The people were
really nice and made me feel special. This taught me a
lot about God's love.

I never found a new church "home" when we moved
to a larger city, so I missed the peace and love I had
experienced. Thankfully, God placed loving Christians
in my path who were praying for me. This helped me
feel safe, even though my home was not.

I couldn't have endured the pain without Christ and
the loving people He brought into my life. He guided
and protected me and was by my side even when I did
not prioritize my relationship with Him. I know that
no matter what anyone thinks of me, I am special to my
heavenly Father. He has shown His love to me through
the family of God.

Do you know someone you need to reach out to or who is reach-
ing out to you? Ask God to help you go beyond the exterior so
that you can see Christ in them.

SAFE WITH SPIRITUAL FAMILY

When we turn our lives over to God, trust that He is for us, and
see Christ in those around us, He brings people into our lives to
become members of our spiritual family. The bond between two
believers can be stronger than biological family because they are
bound together with the priceless blood of the Lamb (Proverbs
18:24).

We see this truth revealed in the life of Christ. One day when
Jesus was speaking to a large crowd, His mother and brothers
came looking for Him. When He was told they were outside He
said to the crowd, "'Who is my mother? Who are my brothers?'

Then he pointed to his disciples and said, 'Look, these are my mother and brothers. Anyone who does the will of my Father in heaven is my brother and sister and mother!'" (Matthew 12:48-50). Jesus had a loving relationship with His followers and adopted them as His spiritual family.

The Holy One desires to place us in a spiritual family as well, but we must be the ones to develop bonds of love in these relationships. This requires taking the risk of being hurt, even though it goes against our nature. We must acknowledge that we need His divine intervention to become vitally connected with our new family members. They can become a safe place for us so that we no longer need to hide.

One of the most important things we can do to become a safe place for our spiritual family is to be careful with our words. Although the tongue is a very small part of the body, it is extremely powerful. In fact, it's the strongest muscle in the body in proportion to its size and can cause damage when used as a weapon. A well-contained fire can provide warmth on a cold evening, light in a dark room, nourishment when something is cooked over it, and beauty on a dreary day—but when that same fire gets out of control it can harm, destroy, and even kill. The same thing is true about our words:

> So also the tongue is a small thing, but what enormous damage it can do. A great forest can be set on fire by one tiny spark. And the tongue is a flame of fire. It is full of wickedness, and poisons every part of the body. And the tongue is set on fire by hell itself and can turn our whole lives into a blazing flame of destruction and disaster.
>
> Men have trained, or can train, every kind of animal or bird that lives and every kind of reptile and fish, but no human being can tame the tongue. It is always ready to pour out its deadly poison. Sometimes it praises our

heavenly Father, and sometimes it breaks out into curses
against men who are made like God. And so blessing
and cursing come pouring out of the same mouth. Dear
brothers, surely this is not right!

JAMES 3:5-10, TLB

We have a choice to make with our speech. We can use it to nourish, bless, and give life to others, or we can curse them with caus-
tic words. Our words have the power to bestow praise, approval,
protection, preservation, and favor upon those we love—and the
power to inflict hurt and evil.

Blessings and curses are incompatible, but far too often
they exist together. Our desire is to bless, but we get frustrated
and angry, and before we know it angry words spew out of our
mouths. It takes the power of the Holy Spirit to keep our tongue
from saying something cruel. As we draw closer to the Lord, His
love will flow through us and we will give out blessings instead
of curses.

We all mess up from time to time, so don't lose heart when
this happens. Just apologize and replace the curse with a blessing.
Remember that these loved ones are your spiritual family, and
give them a safe place to experience relationship.

REVERSE HIDE AND SEEK

I love Dennis and Barbara Rainey's story about an interesting
game that helps their family experience community:

One of our favorite games that our children absolutely
loved playing was Reverse Hide and Seek. We'd turn
out all the lights in our house. Then, instead of having
one person look for everyone else, one person hid and
all the others would try to find him or her. When you
located the hidden person, you would quietly slip into

the same space to hide with him or her. The game would keep going until only one person was left seeking all the others in a pitch black, totally silent house.

It wasn't easy being the last man standing. Swiftly, the house would become very quiet and still. All you could hear was the sound of your own panting and your appeals for everyone to show themselves. But usually, the giggles and snickers of seven people huddling in the bathtub or under a table would give away their location. When the last person finally joined the crowd, it was a huge relief—almost like a family reunion, full of laughter, hugs and silly recaps of the highlights.[3]

The game of Reverse Hide and Seek is a great illustration of what the Holy One desires for His children. Instead of hiding from one another, we should seek to connect our hearts in an intimate way. We need to huddle together and rejoice in the fact that we are doing life together. No one should have to face the world alone in the family of God.

I have spent most of my life hiding my true self from others, but by God's grace I am being transformed. I am experiencing deeper intimacy with God, and I'm finding that the two greatest commandments go hand in hand. The more intimate I become with my Beloved, the closer I become with people. And the closer I become with people, the more intimate I become with my Beloved. By giving myself fully to God and to others, I am finding joy.

Are you ready to step out in faith and play the game of Reverse Hide and Seek? In this place you can come out of your hiding place and experience healing in community.

And may the Lord make your love for one another and for all people grow and overflow, just as our love for you overflows. May he, as a result, make your hearts strong, blameless, and holy as you stand before God our Father when our Lord Jesus comes again with all his holy people.   1 THESSALONIANS 3:12-13

THE GARDEN OF GETHSEMANE STUDY

DAY 1: HIDING PLACES

1. Are you satisfied with your relationships with other people? If not, how would you like to see them change? What do you need to do in order for this to happen?

2. Have you ever been afraid to develop a close relationship with another person even though they seemed to be safe? If so, explain what happened.

3. Read Genesis 3:1-10. Using the game Hide and Seek, paraphrase these verses so that a child can understand.

4. What can we replace our walls of protection with according to Psalm 5:11-12? What do you need to do for this to happen?

5. Spend time worshiping and record your thoughts here or in a journal. (Optional worship verses: Psalm 56:3 and 56:13.)

DAY 2: THE GREAT COMMANDMENTS

1. When asked about the greatest commandment, what was Jesus' answer in Matthew 22:36-40? Why do you think He added the second greatest commandment?

2. What does Matthew 22:40 say about all the commandments? Why do you think this is true? (Hint: Read the Ten Commandments in Deuteronomy 5:7-21.)

3. What level of communication are most of your relationships in? (See page 168.) Is this satisfying? If not, what do you need to change? Explain your answer.

4. Read John 13:34. What is the new commandment and how is it different from the old one?

5. Is this new commandment easier or harder for you to obey? Explain your answer.

6. Read Romans 12:9-10. Are you loving others in this way? If not, what do you need to change? Give an example of someone who has loved you like this or someone you have loved in this way.

7. Spend time in worship and record your thoughts here or in a journal. (Optional worship verses: Psalm 26:3 and Psalm 27:4.)

DAY 3: THE SOURCE OF THIS NEW KIND OF LOVE

1. We all crave genuine loving relationships where we can find a place to belong. Thankfully, this new kind of love does not depend on us. Read Romans 15:30, 1 Thessalonians 3:12, and 1 Thessalonians 4:9. What do these verses reveal about the source of this kind of love? What is your response to this truth?

2. The source of this new kind of love is supernatural, but we also have a part to play. Read Galatians 5:22. What does it mean for the Holy Spirit to control your life? What are the results? What does this look like for you personally?

3. This new kind of love requires connecting with others even though we risk being hurt. The apostle Paul understood this very well. Read 2 Corinthians 12:15 and try to put yourself in his shoes. What emotions do you think he was feeling? What was his attitude about the rejection from the Corinthians? What can we learn from this?

4. In 2 Corinthians 6:11-13 Paul took the risk of loving others even though they had rejected him. Have you experienced this kind of rejection in the past? How did you respond? What can we learn from the way Paul handled this situation?

5. When we finally understand that the heart of God is for our good, we can transfer this to our relationships

with others and find a few safe people. Read Romans
8:28-33 and describe how this changes your attitude about
relationships.

DAY 4: SURPRISED BY THE REFLECTION

1. As believers we are one with the Holy One. Explain what
the mystery or secret is in Colossians 1:24-28 and who it is
intended for. What impact does this have on your life?

2. When we accept Christ as our personal Savior, something
miraculous happens. Read Galatians 2:20 and explain it in
a way that a child can understand.

3. When we look with spiritual eyes into the hearts of our
loved ones, we are surprised by the reflection of Christ.
Read Colossians 2:2 and explain how our relationships
would change if we practiced this on a consistent basis.

4. The Bible reveals that God brings people into our lives to
become special members of our eternal family. Read John
19:26-27 and explain what happened in these verses. Why
do you think Jesus did this? How do you think this made
John and Mary feel?

5. Read 1 Peter 1:22. What are the believers called in this verse? What are they encouraged to do and why? Do you love others in this way?

6. Spend time in worship and record your thoughts here or in a journal. (Optional worship verses: Psalm 73:23-26).

DAY 5: SAFE WITH SPIRITUAL FAMILY

1. In order to become a safe place for others, we must be careful with our words. Read Ephesians 4:2. How does this admonition relate to the way we speak to others?

2. We can use our speech to nourish, bless, and give life to others. Read Ephesians 4:29 and personalize it. How well are you applying this verse? What can you do to improve in this area?

3. We can also use our speech to injure, harass, torment, and bring death to others. What happens to the person in Psalm 64:2-8 who curses others with his words? What can you do to improve in this area?

4. All of us make mistakes at times with our speech. What does 1 Peter 4:8 encourage us to do when we mess up? Give an example of this in your life.

5. What is the result of community according to Romans
   15:5-7? Are you glorifying God in your relationships? What
   do you need to change in order to enjoy greater harmony
   with believers that God has placed in your life?

6. Read Psalm 59:16-17 and worship the Holy One. Record
   your thoughts here or in a journal.

CHAPTER 10

THE SHELTER
OF THE MOST HIGH

"I WANT MY PAPPY! I WANT MY PAPPY! I WAANNNT MYYYY PAAAPPYY!!" my three-year-old grandson shrieked as we wound our way through the crowded shopping mall. We had just had a delightful time watching Greyson make a "Pappy Monkey" at Build-A-Bear. Greyson had a big smile on his face as he watched the white stuffing fill the monkey he chose, and the smile grew even bigger as he carefully squeezed his beloved Pappy (pacifier) into the stuffed monkey before it was stitched together. But this rite of passage suddenly morphed into chaotic confusion when we walked out of the store. He hurled his new monkey as far as he could and continually screamed at the top of his lungs, "I WANT MY PAPPY!" The adults in our party were sheepishly giggling as people stared at the wailing toddler.

Greyson could be easily soothed when he was awake or asleep as long as he had the comfort of his pacifier, so it was rough for the whole family when it was no longer available. His parents weren't trying to play a cruel trick on him; they simply knew that it was past time for him to give his pacifier up. Growing up meant he had to learn other ways to manage his distress.

I can be a lot like Greyson. Because of the trauma in my past I've had my own pappies that I've sought comfort from. A continual sense of restlessness kept me striving to find something or someone that might provide some relief, but nothing worked. I was on the verge of giving up, when much to my surprise, my broken road led me to the heart of God, where I am experiencing true rest. Now I am able to find healing comfort in the Shelter of the Most High. In this place of safety, God is always with me and I'm able to return to joy as I relax in His loving arms:

> Those who live in the shelter of the Most High
> 　　will find rest in the shadow of the Almighty.
> This I declare about the LORD:
> He alone is my refuge, my place of safety;
> 　　he is my God, and I trust him.

PSALM 91:1-2

THE DIVINE ACHE

I love these words from Saint Augustine: "Thou hast formed us for Thyself, and our hearts are restless till they find rest in Thee."[1] Augustine understood that there is a cry in each of us for something that will fill the inner longing of our souls. We enter the world crying for love and attention, and then we search for someone or something to fill this divine ache. What we don't realize is that we are born with a desire to drink deeply from the One who calls Himself "Living Water." The psalmist understood this longing: "I lift my hands to you in prayer. I thirst for you as parched land thirsts for rain" (Psalm 143:6).

We were made for intimacy with God, but sin left us in pain, isolation, and confusion. Like Adam and Eve, we have been duped into believing that we can find permanent satisfaction in temporal things—but we are only left with an even deeper longing.

THE DIVINE SOLUTION

There is a divine solution to this problem. Jesus promised that we can experience abundant life here on earth that will fill this divine ache: "I assure you that everyone who has given up house or wife or brothers or parents or children, for the sake of the Kingdom of God, will be repaid many times over in this life, and will have eternal life in the world to come" (Luke 18:29-30). These verses promise healing comfort and joy for you and me in this life. That means that we don't have to wait until heaven to experience this amazing gift. There is a place of rest in the Shelter of the Most High. It is a fountain overflowing with spiritual refreshment, but finding rest in this place of refuge is not an easy task.

There is a well-known passage of Scripture that is often used as an invitation for people to know Christ as their personal Savior: "Behold, I stand at the door and knock; if anyone hears My voice and opens the door, I will come in to him and will dine with him, and he with Me" (Revelation 3:20, NASB). This verse reveals, as we have seen throughout our journey together so far, that Jesus is a gentleman and will never force Himself upon us. He knocks and patiently waits for us to invite Him in. Our initial step is to open our hearts to Christ as Savior, but far too often we get stuck there and never move to the deeper level of communion. Throughout our Christian walk, Christ is always waiting patiently for us to intimately "dine with Him."

The Shelter of the Most High is where we commune with our Beloved in a way that satisfies the soul hunger we were born with. A. W. Tozer describes it in this way: "It's the will of God that I should press on to be united with Him in the warmth of personal knowledge of a union that leads to communion. A sweet fellowship and a harmony with God that is wonderful, that makes this Earth a Heaven, and brings the Heaven yonder a lot closer."[2]

WHAT THE SHELTER ISN'T
Walls

I asked Christ to come into my life when I was in college, but then I shut the door to the deeper place of intimacy because I was afraid to be known. As a result, I had a wall of protection around my heart that brought some relief for a while, but never true rest. In time I recognized that this wall made me feel alone, afraid, and exhausted. I needed to give Jesus permission to come in to the deeper places that I had shut off to everyone, including Him.

In the book of John we see a miraculous encounter between Jesus and a lame man who had been lying by the Pool of Bethesda for thirty-eight years, desiring to be healed: "When Jesus saw him and knew he had been ill for a long time, he asked him, 'Would you like to get well?'" (John 5:6). That seems like an obvious question with an obvious answer, but instead of answering the question, the man gave an excuse. He told Jesus that healing wasn't possible for him because he couldn't get to the water in time. Like many of us, this man had a limited view of healing.

At the beginning of my healing journey Jesus asked me, "Bev, would you like to get well?" Instead of answering this question I gave an excuse: "Healing isn't possible for me because I'm afraid to let my walls down." Then Jesus said, "Will you allow Me to get past your walls and go into the deeper places of your heart so that I can heal you?" I could hardly bear to think about life without my protective walls, so I thought long and hard and responded hesitantly, "I guess so, but it's going to hurt, isn't it?" Jesus gently said, "Yes, dear one. It's always painful when walls are torn down, but I promise that I will be with you each step of the way. That means that you won't ever be lonely or afraid again. Never, ever!"

Now that was a promise I couldn't resist!

Stasi Eldredge understands about walls of protection. She candidly describes the way God breaks through them: "He knocks through our loneliness. He knocks through our sorrows.

He knocks through events that feel too close to what happened to us when we were young—a betrayal, a rejection, a word spoken, a relationship lost. He knocks through many things, waiting for us to give him permission to enter in."[3]

After being in the pilot study of *Return to Joy*, my friend Nan texted me with this insight: "We need to have such deep intimacy with God that if He says He wants to do open heart surgery on us to break down our self-protective defense mechanisms, we need to say 'Okay, I know You.'" Nan is learning that God's heart is for her good so she can trust Him no matter what. And in the Shelter of the Most High, we can do the same.

Idols

Spiritual maturity that results in deep intimacy with God cannot happen until we are weaned from our idols—anything we are depending on for fulfillment other than the Holy One (1 John 5:21).

We usually think of an idol as an inanimate object used as a foreign god. This was true in Old Testament times, but today's idols are far more sophisticated. Joy Dawson says that "an idol is something or someone that takes a priority place in our lives over the Lord Jesus Christ in our thinking, in our time, in our affection, in our loyalty and in our obedience."[4] We must wean ourselves from any idols before we can experience rest in the Holy One.

King David understood this principle of weaning: "Surely I have composed and quieted my soul; like a weaned child rests against his mother, my soul is like a weaned child within me" (Psalm 131:2, NASB). While you may think that a nursing infant is a perfect picture of rest, a baby is usually fitful and anxious until they latch onto their mother's breast, their main source of sustenance. Complete satisfaction only occurs when their tummy is full. Weaning a child is the first step toward independence from the mother. Because nourishment can come from other sources, a weaned child can rest quietly in her mother's lap.

In the beginning of my healing journey, God provided a couple of amazing women to help me navigate the rough places on the broken road. These godly mentors provided wise counsel and loving comfort while I cried like a baby in their arms. I enjoyed the nurturing I received from them, even though it was foreign to me at first. They were a precious gift from God during this horrific season of my journey, and I grew to love these spiritual mothers deeply. Nevertheless, I continued to feel restless and fitful at times because I was tremendously afraid that they would abandon me. Eventually I realized that I was depending on them, instead of on the Lord, for the abiding comfort I needed. Even though they always directed me to God, in my weakness I allowed them to become an idol in my life.

In my dependency on these women, I had mistakenly become like the Israelites who sought military help from Egypt instead of the Lord: "This is what the Sovereign LORD, the Holy One of Israel, says: 'Only in returning to me and resting in me will you be saved. In quietness and confidence is your strength. But you would have none of it'" (Isaiah 30:15). These dear women could not give me what I longed for: the abundant life that Jesus offers. I needed to transfer my dependence from them to the only One who could be with me 24/7.

Weaning is usually a painful process, but it must happen so we can grow and mature. We cannot find rest in the Shelter of the Most High as long as we are resting in the shelter of someone else. God is honored when we look to Him as our ultimate source of joy and strength. Abba wants us to understand to the fullest extent Paul's words: "This same God who takes care of me will supply *all* your needs from his glorious riches, which have been given to us in Christ Jesus" (Philippians 4:19, emphasis added).

Giving up the things we seek for comfort can be a grueling process. But in time, God helps us see that our daily provision doesn't depend on anything or anyone but Him. We can enjoy the wonderful people He's brought into our lives without depending on them for fulfillment. Others will let us down, but God is always faithful.

Is there anything that has prominence in your life over the Holy One? Is there something or someone that has become an addiction or an idol, supplanting God in your affections? Are you willing to make a choice to press into the Lord as your ultimate source of life, joy, and strength? You will never experience rest until you surrender everything to Him.

WHAT THE SHELTER IS

A Place of Intimate Communion

The Pharisees of Jesus' day looked very religious on the outside, but Jesus told them that they never heard His Father's voice (John 5:37). They enjoyed a legalistic list of dos and don'ts instead of a loving relationship with the living God. They were passionate about God's laws instead of being passionate about God. Far too often we fall into the same pattern. Without realizing it, we believe that gaining more head knowledge or following the rules is the way to know God. But it's only a way to know *about* Him. We mistakenly choose a religious method over vibrant intimacy with the God of the universe.

Three words in the Hebrew language will help us understand more fully what intimacy means. The first is *yada*, which means "to know"[5] and indicates a desire to know the heart of another person. David used this word in Psalm 139:1 when he said, "O LORD, You have searched me and known me" (NASB).

The next Hebrew word is *sod*, which means "council of familiar conversation."[6] This speaks of vulnerable disclosure, which requires that you allow someone to truly know your heart and mind. Solomon used this word in Proverbs 3:32: "He [God] is intimate with the upright" (NASB).

The third Hebrew word is *sakan*, which means "to be of use, service or profit"[7] and indicates a caring involvement. This type of intimacy is motivated by the desire to help those you are closely involved with. It is also used in Psalm 139: "You . . . are intimately acquainted with all my ways" (verse 3, NASB).

Intimacy between two people should always be for the purpose of doing good and blessing each other. God's motive is never to hurt or embarrass us. We can trust that His heart is for our good and can enjoy the lifelong thrill of searching out the Holy One and becoming more and more intimate with Him as each day passes.

A Place of Rest

Rest. We all want it but can't seem to find it. When Moses requested to be intimately connected to the Lord, God promised, "My presence shall go with you, and I will give you rest" (Exodus 33:14, NASB). But can we experience rest in the hectic world in which we live? Yes—but only when we understand what an intimate relationship with God looks like.

We all have two different kinds of relationships: acquaintances and intimate friends. Acquaintances are those we don't know very well. We feel the need to entertain them and are careful to make them feel comfortable. While we may enjoy them, we are never able to fully relax.

But what about intimate friends? These people are more like family members. We've spent countless hours together and we know each other's hearts well. We have a relaxed relationship and are not anxious with moments of silence. We experience deep intimacy and can sometimes tell what the other is thinking. It's possible to know God in this way, but it takes time to develop.

Like many, Beth learned this lesson the hard way:

An unmarried teenage mother in my home! I was devastated . . . not because of what my daughter would have to go through, but because it would mar the way our wonderful Christian family looked to others. I had been saved by grace, but this didn't fit into my plans.

Then I realized that Jesus is "in me," and He isn't afraid . . . so I don't have to be afraid either. Gradually I learned how to live without the paralyzing fear of mistakes, rejection, and loss of control that was so much a part of my life. I also learned to surrender things I thought were my rights: the right to be in control of my life, the right to take offense, and the right to be right.

God taught me to learn to rest in Him. He has set me on a journey that will continue to grow richer and sweeter until I meet Him face to face.

Beth was able to cease from striving for perfection as she drew near to the heart of God. Are you closer to the heart of God now than you were a year ago? Can you find rest in His presence and enjoy deep intimacy?

A Place of Joyous Celebration

God has issued an invitation to His children to rejoice in every moment of life because every moment of life is a gift—but by now you know the saga. Our Beloved offers a gift, but the adversary relentlessly tries to steal it from us. Jesus promises an abundant life filled with His joy, but the evil one tries to break our hearts and destroy our lives with grief. What are we to do? Nehemiah said to the grieving Israelites, "Go and celebrate with a feast of rich foods and sweet drinks, and share gifts of food with people who have nothing prepared. This is a sacred day before our Lord. Don't be dejected and sad, for the joy of the LORD is your strength!" (Nehemiah 8:10).

Joy is an important aspect of the spiritual life. God is full of joy and desires for His creation to reflect His pleasure. Jesus said, "These things I have spoken to you so that My joy may be in you, and that your joy may be made full" (John 15:11, NASB). While we cannot manufacture joy on our own, the fact that Jesus is with me means that His joy can fill me even in the midst of uncertain circumstances.

A joyful spirit can be cultivated by celebrating the goodness of God. This was the primary focus of the festivals in the Old Testament. These times of feasting were always centered on worshiping the Lord. They were meant to be life-changing experiences characterized by sincere thankfulness and jubilant rejoicing.

Each time we go into God's presence in worship, we have the opportunity to participate in a time of holy and joyful celebration. Even when we are in the midst of deep trials, we can exercise our spiritual senses so that we're in touch with His abundant blessings. Worship enables us to take great delight in something that we would have probably overlooked otherwise.

Are you celebrating the gifts the Holy One has given you? Are you spending time in worship, rejoicing in Him? He has invited you into the Shelter of the Most High where His joy is overflowing.

A Place of Restoration

The Shelter of the Most High is a place of breathtaking restoration. We may wonder how we can be restored after so much pain, abuse, and neglect—and Luke has an answer for us: "The Son of Man has come to seek and to save that which was lost" (Luke 19:10, NASB). Jesus has rescued us from the evil one and restored all that he tried to steal from us. We can find comfort in the embrace of our heavenly Father who heals our broken hearts.

This restoration includes the gift of a new name:

The nations will see your righteousness,
And all kings your glory;
And you will be called by a new name
Which the mouth of the LORD will designate.
You will also be a crown of beauty in the hand of the LORD,
And a royal diadem in the hand of your God.
It will no longer be said to you, "Forsaken,"
Nor to your land will it any longer be said, "Desolate";
But you will be called, "My delight is in her,"
And your land, "Married";
For the LORD delights in you,
And to Him your land will be married.
For as a young man marries a virgin,
So your sons will marry you;
And as the bridegroom rejoices over the bride,
So your God will rejoice over you.

ISAIAH 62:2-5, NASB

This promise was for Israel, but God has adopted us into His family and bestowed upon us a new name. Satan tries to steal this truth from us, but our Beloved proves His love over and over again. I was branded "Unwanted" as a child, but my new name is "Beloved Daughter." Now I am sure, without a doubt, that I belong to the Holy One. I am my Beloved's and He is mine, and no power in heaven, earth, or hell can ever change that fact.

Candy also experienced restoration from the Lord:

Once upon a time there was a teenage girl named
Candy who became pregnant. She solved this problem
by aborting her baby and convincing herself that this
was a good decision. In the years that followed, Candy
got married and gave birth to two children. Her strong
maternal love for them began stirring feelings of

anguish over her decision to abort her first child. This
anguish was accompanied by a deep sense of shame that
prevented her from seeking help.

Years passed. Then one day Candy sensed the Lord
urging her to let others know about her abortion.
No one in her present life knew, except her husband,
and the thought of exposing this horrible secret was
terrifying.

After many tears, she finally told her teenaged
children. Next she told her fellow board members of the
local crisis pregnancy center. Then she joined a post-
abortion Bible study that God used to set her free from
the shame she had borne for so long. Jesus so utterly and
completely healed and delivered her, it was as though she
had never had an abortion.

I have shared my story in the third person because it seems like
it happened to someone else. Years have passed since Jesus set me
free, and He has kept me free (John 8:36)!

Have you experienced this kind of restorative power? It
doesn't matter what you've done or what's been done to you—
God desires to restore all that has been lost, including your innocence. He wants to give you a new name so that you are no longer
defined by your past:

> To all who mourn in Israel,
>   he will give a crown of beauty for ashes,
> a joyous blessing instead of mourning,
>   festive praise instead of despair.
> In their righteousness, they will be like
>   great oaks
>   that the LORD has planted for his own glory.

ISAIAH 61:3

HEALED

On a cold, dark morning several years ago, my friend Tina came across a wounded male feral cat that looked like he had been run over and was almost dead. Tina frantically took it to the vet's office, where she was informed that attempting to save the cat would be a waste of time and money . . . but she begged them to try anyway. To everyone's amazement, the cat slowly made progress, and finally Tina got a call saying that he was well enough to be released. The vet told her that the cat could never become tame because he was too wild and too old, so she should drop him off by a barn in the country.

Tina believed that this banged-up feral cat was worth saving, so she begged her husband to let her try to tame him. He agreed, and they took him home and named him Tigger. They placed Tigger in a back bedroom with food and water, where Tina worked with him each morning and evening. At first he hid from her, but in time, much to her amazement, he came out of hiding. He wouldn't allow her to touch him or get very close, but still . . . he was warming up to her. She grew to love him more each day, even though he was skittish and took so much of her time.

After many months Tigger began to eat out of Tina's hand, and then he let her hold him. Twice a day she cuddled him gently for an hour and loved on him. Finally Tigger was able to rest peacefully in her arms. Now he is her favorite pet and they both find great joy snuggling together.

Some of us have been much like Tigger, wild and deeply wounded on the inside. We ran and hid from Jesus at first, but He gave us the space we needed, and in time He showed us that we were His beloved daughters. He healed our wounds as we learned to nestle into His lap and allowed Him to safely love on us. Jesus' romantic betrothal and the Holy Spirit's tender nurturing can soothe all of our relational wounds. God wants to bring us out of the darkness and into the light where we are no longer lonely and afraid. He is always with us, helping us return to joy. We can rest peacefully in His embrace because He loved us enough to tame us.

In the midst of our pain, we have the opportunity to know Jesus in a way that causes us to treasure our journey as one of God's dearest gifts. By His mercy and grace, Abba can take the ugly things in our lives and transform them into something beautiful.

The Holy One is asking, "Will you come to My shelter and find rest? I am waiting patiently for you."

I waited patiently for the LORD to help me,
    and he turned to me and heard my cry.
He lifted me out of the pit of despair,
    out of the mud and the mire.
He set my feet on solid ground
    and steadied me as I walked along.
He has given me a new song to sing,
    a hymn of praise to our God.
Many will see what he has done and be amazed.
    They will put their trust in the LORD.

PSALM 40:1-3

THE SHELTER OF THE MOST HIGH STUDY

DAY 1: THE DIVINE ACHE

1. What is the Shelter of the Most High according to Psalm 91? Make a list of the benefits of this shelter listed in this psalm.

2. Do you personally agree with the statement "There is a cry in each of us for something that will fill the inner longing of our souls"? (See page 186.) Explain why or why not.

3. Read Psalm 130:5-6 and explain it so that a child can understand. (In ancient times guards or watchmen had the grueling assignment of guarding a city all night long.) Have you experienced this kind of ache? What have you tried to fill your soul hunger with? What were the results?

4. Jesus promised that we can experience abundant life that will fill this divine ache. Read Psalm 27:13. What promise was the psalmist looking forward to? How does this encourage your heart?

5. In what ways has God personally provided fulfillment for your soul hunger? Explain your answer.

6. Spend twenty minutes (or as many as you can) in worship and record your thoughts here or in a journal. (Optional worship verses: Psalm 84.)

DAY 2: WHAT THE SHELTER ISN'T

1. Are you stuck in your spiritual walk, or have you allowed Christ to go past any walls to the deeper places of your heart? Explain your answer.

2. In John 5:6 Jesus asked a lame man an important question: "Would you like to get well?" (See page 188.) What would your answer be to this question and why?

3. Are you willing to allow the Lord to tear down your walls so that the He can fill up the longing of your soul? Please be honest! Read Philippians 4:19. How can you apply this verse in this situation?

4. What does Deuteronomy 4:23 say about God? Write this in a way that a child can understand.

5. True intimacy cannot happen until we are weaned from anything we are depending on for fulfillment besides the Holy One. What does God's Word say about fulfillment in Psalm 90:14-15?

6. Is there something in your life that has become an idol? What is it and what do you need to do with it?

7. Joshua warned the Israelites about worshiping idols in Joshua 24:14-27 and then they set up a memorial stone as a witness of the choice they made. Read this account and decide if you are willing to worship the Lord alone as the Israelites did. If you are, make a memorial marker of some kind to be a reminder of the choice you are making today. Describe it here. (It can be as simple as writing on a rock.)

DAY 3: WHAT THE SHELTER IS

1. In Hebrews 11:6 and Psalm 9:9-10, what are the promises for those who seek God?

2. There are many verses that teach that we can be secure in Christ's love. Ephesians 3:17 says, "May Christ through your faith [actually] dwell (settle down, abide, make His permanent home) in your hearts! May you be rooted deep in love and founded securely on love"

(Ephesians 3:17, AMPC). Use this verse to write a prayer asking the Lord to fill up your life with His presence.

3. What instruction did the Lord give the Israelites in Jeremiah 6:16, and what was their reply? What would be your honest response to the instruction and why?

4. Read Psalm 62:1-2, 5-8. What do these verses imply about rest?

5. Read Isaiah 26:3-4, 12-13 and personalize them here. What are you doing to apply these verses? Explain your answer.

6. Spend twenty minutes (or as many as you can) in worship and record your thoughts here or in a journal. (Optional worship verse: Psalm 75:1.)

DAY 4: A PLACE OF JOYOUS CELEBRATION

1. Read Isaiah 52:9 and Ecclesiastes 5:20. Have you experienced this kind of comfort from the Lord? If you have, explain what happened and how you responded.

2. Read Psalm 27:5-6 and Psalm 70:4 and personalize them here.

3. Read Psalm 69:30-34 and record your thoughts here or in a journal. Spend time celebrating in the presence of the Holy One.

4. The Lord is a God of restoration. Read Jeremiah 31:12-13. What was the message to the children of Israel? How can this be applied in your life?

5. What was God's message to the children of Israel in Isaiah 58:8? How can you apply this in your life? Think about what you've learned during this study.

6. Read Psalm 102:17-22 and Psalm 30:11-12 and make a list of all the things these verses say the Lord accomplishes. Have you experienced any of these in your life? Explain your answer.

7. God's restoration includes the gift of a new name. Read Isaiah 62:2-5 and explain what happened so that a child can understand. God gave Jerusalem a new name and He has a new name for you, too. Spend time in worship and ask Him to tell you what it is. Record your thoughts here or in a journal.

DAY 5: HEALED

1. How has your relationship with God changed since you began this study?

2. Walking the broken road to intimacy leads to the heart of God. Read Proverbs 3:6 and explain how you will know which path to take when you've finished this study.

3. Read Jeremiah 31:35-37 and think of all the Holy One has done for you while walking the broken road to intimacy. Worship Him and record your thoughts here or in a journal.

How to Use the Study

RETURN TO JOY differs from most Bible studies in that it is designed to encourage women to journey to the healing presence of the Holy One through God's Word, reflection on personal experiences, and individual worship. This ten-week study can be done in a group, with a friend or counselor, or by yourself. Each lesson is divided into five days, including a time for daily individual worship. It is very important to make this worship time a priority, because this is where healing can take place.

Many of the questions will guide you into Scripture passages. Ask God to reveal His truth to you through His Word. Other questions will ask you to reflect on your own personal life. Ask the Holy One to help you answer these questions honestly and thoughtfully, even if it's painful. When this study was field-tested, I was amazed by the significant impact our ten weeks together had on each person. God can do the same for you if you open your heart to all that He has for you.

INSTRUCTIONS FOR GROUP LEADERS

Research shows that the main reason people drop out of a group is because they don't feel safe, or they feel they don't belong. Therefore, your job as a facilitator for the small group is a vital one. You are not a teacher—your role is to humbly help the members look into the Word; provide a safe, nonjudgmental environment for sharing what they are learning; and lovingly guide them so that they will feel welcome in the group. Ask the Holy One to help you create an environment for authentic, heartfelt communication where no masks are needed.

The lessons are designed so that participants will spend about fifteen minutes a day in Bible study and up to twenty minutes a day in worship. (The worship times begin with chapter 3.) Women will get the most out of the study if they can write their answers to the questions ahead of time and go deep with God in daily worship. However, remember that each group member is unique. Some women may not be able to complete every question. Don't discourage them from attending or contributing if they haven't finished their lesson. There is no place for shame in this study! Twenty minutes of worship a day is a goal, not a demand.

When the group gathers to discuss the study, it's enough to let one or two women answer the questions about what the Bible passages say. It's not necessary to go around the circle and hear each person's answer. But it can be fruitful to let as many women as possible share their answers to the questions about their own lives. They can pass if they like, but they should always have the opportunity to share what they wrote. It should take about ninety minutes to discuss each week's lesson.

Never discourage tears as the women share in the study. Tears are cleansing and should always be welcomed. Provide tissues throughout the room so that they can be easily accessible when needed.

Don't be afraid of silence. Women may be gathering their courage to share something deeply personal. Or they may be thinking about what someone else shared and letting their own thoughts form.

Worship is an essential part of this study, so I encourage you to end each lesson with worship. Women should be encouraged to spread out in the room so that they can comfortably express their love to the Holy One as worship music is played softly in the background. Suggested songs for each chapter are provided on the Return to Joy website.

Maintaining confidentiality is key to the success of a study of this nature. Everyone in the group needs to agree not to communicate information shared to anyone outside the group unless they have permission to do so. (I tell the women in my study that I hold the sensitive things they tell me as a treasure in my heart.)

The most important thing you can do for your group is to use your spiritual senses to hear what the Holy One desires for each member of the class. If your heart is tender toward the leading of the Holy Spirit, He will use you in a powerful way to guide others in their healing journeys.

The Bridge to Life

ONE OF THE OLDEST QUESTIONS humankind has been asking is, "How can I know God?" The question is a valid one. What is He like? What can we do to please Him? How can we get to Heaven? If we work hard enough to be a good enough person, will He accept us then? If we do enough religious activities to get His attention, will that do it?

Fortunately for us, the answer is surprisingly simple. The "Gospel" that the Bible talks about literally means, "the Good News," and the news is good indeed!

First, we have to start at the beginning. In Genesis 1:26, when God created the first humans, He said, "Let us make mankind in our image, in our likeness," then God blessed them and spent the days walking and talking with the people He had created. In short, life was good.

But why isn't life like that anymore? What happened to mess everything up? This brings us to the second point: when we (humankind) chose to do the opposite of what God told us, sin poisoned the world. Sin separated us from God, and everything changed. Romans 3:23 says, "For all have sinned and fall short of the glory of God," and in Isaiah 59:2 we're told, "Your iniquities have separated you from your God; your sins have hidden his face from you so that he will not hear."

This is especially bad news because there is no way for us to get across that gap on our own. We (humankind) have tried to find our way back to God and a perfect world on our own ever since then, and without any luck. We try to get there by being good people, or through religion, money, morality, philosophy, education, or any number of other ways, but eventually we find out that none of it works. "There is a way that seems right to a man, but in the end it leads to death" (Proverbs 14:12).

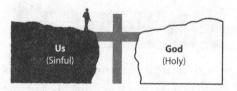

There is only one way to find peace with God, and the Bible says it is through Jesus Christ. We were stranded without any way of getting back to our Creator, and we needed a way to pay for our sins and be clean again so that we could be welcomed back to be with Him. Romans 5:8 says, "But God demonstrates His own love for us in this: While we were still sinners, Christ died for us." So this is the Good News—that even though we were still enemies of God (as one translation says), Jesus came to die on the cross and pay the price for our sins so that we could have a relationship with Him again. John 3:16 says, "For God so loved the world that He gave His one and only son, that whoever believes in Him shall not perish but have eternal life."

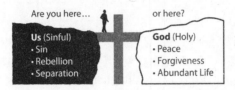

What then should be our reaction to this awesome news? This brings us to the last and most important part. John 5:24 says, "I tell you the truth, whoever hears my word and believes Him who sent me has eternal life and will not be condemned; he has crossed over from death to life." Jesus Christ himself even says, "I have come that they may have life, and have it to the full" (John 10:10), and Romans 5:1 says, "We have peace with God through our Lord Jesus Christ."

So how can I have peace with God, life to the full, and be confident of eternal life like these verses say? First, through an honest prayer to God, I have to admit that I'm not perfect—that I can't escape my sins, and I can't save myself. I follow this admission by believing that Jesus Christ died for me on the cross and rose from the grave, conquering death and sin. Then I invite Jesus Christ to live in me and be the Lord of my life, accepting His free gift of eternal life with Him.

The prayer can go something like this:

> *Dear Jesus,*
>
> *I know that I am a sinner and that I need You to forgive me. I know that You died a painful death so that my sins could be washed clean. Thank you. I want to make You the Lord of my life, and I will trust and follow You. Everything I have is Yours now.*
>
> *In Your name, Lord.*
>
> *Amen.*

There is nothing magical about these words. It's not the words themselves that make things right between you and God—it's whether or not your heart really means it. We know this because in 1 Samuel 16:7, the Bible says, "The LORD does not look at the things people look at. People look at the outward appearance, but the Lord looks at the heart."

The best part of this whole process is that it doesn't matter how badly we've messed up, Jesus is powerful enough to save anyone from their sins—even the worst of us. Romans 10:13 says, "Everyone who calls on the name of the Lord will be saved." That's fantastic news—no matter how badly we've messed up, we can place our complete trust in Jesus, and He will wipe all of our sins off the face of the earth. Jesus is the bridge to life.

Notes

CHAPTER 1: WHY THIS JOURNEY?

1. James G. Friesen and others, *The Life Model* (Shepherd's House, 1999), 22.

CHAPTER 2: THE VALLEY OF WEEPING

1. Lisa See, *Snow Flower and the Secret Fan* (New York: Random House, 2005, 2009), 30.
2. Acquaintance rape occurs when a perpetrator uses physical or psychological intimidation to force someone to have sex against their wishes, or when the perpetrator has sex with someone who has been incapacitated by drugs or alcohol. Even if vaginal penetration doesn't occur, when a person is forced to do any sexual acts without their consent, they can experience severe emotional damage. Typically, women believe that if they've been forced to have sexual contact with someone they know, it's less believable and less serious than stranger rape, especially if there has been some level of romantic interest between the attacker and the victim. But even if there has been previous consensual sex, any type of forced sexual activity is assault. See US Department of Justice, *National Crime Victimization Study: 2009–2013*, https://rainn.org/get-information/statistics /sexual-assault-offenders.
3. US Department of Justice, *National Crime Victimization Survey: 2008–2012*, https://rainn.org/get-information/statistics/reporting-rates.

CHAPTER 3: THE GATEWAY OF HOPE

1. A. P. Gibbs, quoted in Linda Dillow, *Satisfy My Thirsty Soul* (Colorado Springs, CO: NavPress, 2007), 45.
2. *The Brown-Driver-Briggs Hebrew and English Lexicon*, Unabridged, Electronic Database, copyright © 2002, 2003, 2006 by Biblesoft, Inc., s.v. "hiph'il."
3. *Thayer's Greek-English Lexicon of the New Testament*, Electronic Database, copyright © 2002, 2003, 2006, 2011 by Biblesoft, Inc., s.v. "proskynéō."
4. Dillow, *Satisfy My Thirsty Soul*, 37.

CHAPTER 4: THE SECRET PLACE

1. *Merriam-Webster's Collegiate Dictionary, Eleventh Edition*, s.v. "intimate."
2. A. W. Tozer, *Gems from Tozer* (Camp Hill, PA: Wingspread, 1979), 15.
3. Jonathan Edwards, *A Treatise Concerning Religious Affections* (Philadelphia: James Crissy, 1821), 16.
4. *Strong's Concordance*, "exult," H7797.

5. *Strong's Concordance*, "rejoice," H1523.
6. Sarah Edwards, quoted in Jonathan Edwards, *The Works of Jonathan Edwards*, Volume 1 (London: John Childs and Son, 1839), cvii.
7. Charla Pereau and James F. Sheer, *Charla's Children* (Minneapolis, MN: Bethany, 1981), 230.

CHAPTER 5: THE BRIDGE TO ROMANCE
1. Dee Brestin and Kathy Troccoli, *Falling in Love with Jesus* (Nashville, TN: Word, 2000), 9.
2. Randy Alcorn, *Heaven* (Carol Stream, IL: Tyndale, 2004), 199.
3. Bob Sorge, *Secrets of the Secret Place* (Grandview, MO: Oasis, 2001), 19.

CHAPTER 6: UNDER HIS SHADOW
1. Jill Briscoe, "A Note from Jill Briscoe," *Just Between Us* Magazine 22.1, Winter 2011, 3.
2. *NAS Exhaustive Concordance of the Bible with Hebrew-Aramaic and Greek Dictionaries*, copyright © 1981, 1998 by the Lockman Foundation, s.v. "el."
3. David Nelmes, "God Is Agape Love," Ezilon Infobase, November 10, 2007, http://www.ezilon.com/articles/articles/7675/1/God-is-Agape-Love.
4. William D. Mounce, *Mounce's Complete Expository Dictionary of Old and New Testament Words*, s.v. "counselor."
5. Hannah Whitall Smith, *God of All Comfort* (Vestal, NY: Anamchara Books, 2011), 56.

CHAPTER 7: THE SHADOW OF DARKNESS
1. Quinn Schipper, *Trading Faces: Dissociation, A Common Solution to Avoiding Life's Pain* (Stillwater, OK: New Forums, 2005), 17.
2. Donald Miller, *Blue Like Jazz* (Nashville, TN: Thomas Nelson, 2003), 86.
3. Alaine Pakkala, *Taking Every Thought Captive: Spiritual Workouts to Help Renew Your Mind in God's Truth* (Colorado Springs, CO: Lydia, 1995), 33.
4. Paul Billheimer, *Destined for the Throne* (Fort Washington, PA: Christian Literature Crusade, 1975), 121.

CHAPTER 8: THE PLACE OF FORGIVENESS
1. *Merriam-Webster's Collegiate Dictionary, Eleventh Edition*, s.v. "offend."
2. John Bevere, *The Bait of Satan* (Lake Mary, FL: Charisma, 2014), 19.
3. *Merriam-Webster's Collegiate Dictionary, Eleventh Edition*, s.v. "forgive."
4. Dan B. Allender, *The Wounded Heart* (Colorado Springs, CO: NavPress, 2008), 219.

CHAPTER 9: THE GARDEN OF GETHSEMANE
1. Mike Mason, *Practicing the Presence of People* (Colorado Springs, CO: Waterbrook, 1999), 16.
2. Cynthia Heald, *Becoming a Woman Who Loves* (Nashville, TN: Thomas Nelson, 2002), xii.

3. Dennis and Barbara Rainey, *Moments with You: 365 All-New Devotions for Couples* (Ventura, CA: Regal, 2007), November 7.

CHAPTER 10: THE SHELTER OF THE MOST HIGH

1. *The Confessions of St. Augustine*, translated by F. J. Sheed (Sheed and Ward, 1942), Book 1, 1.
2. A. W. Tozer, *Fellowship of the Burning Heart* (Alachua, FL: Bridge-Logos, 2006), 93.
3. Stasi Eldredge, *Captivating* (Nashville: Thomas Nelson, 2010), 101.
4. Joy Dawson, *Intimate Friendship with God* (Grand Rapids, MI: Chosen Books, 2008), 148.
5. *Strong's Concordance*, "yada," H3045.
6. *Strong's Concordance*, "sod," H5475.
7. *Strong's Concordance*, "sakan," H5532a.